MW00616131

The Vengeful Heart
and other stories

A true-crime casebook

by
Stephen G. Michaud
And Hugh Aynesworth

*For Lizanne—
who still knows
where the bodies
are buried,

Fondly,

S*

1/12/2001

authorlink press
www.authorlink.com

Published by Authorlink Press
An imprint of Authorlink
(http://www.authorlink.com)
3720 Millswood Dr.
Irving, Texas 75062, USA

First published by Authorlink Press
An imprint of Authorlink
First Printing, December 2000

Copyright © Stephen G. Michaud
  and Hugh Aynesworth, 2000
All rights reserved

Without limiting the rights under copyright reserved above,
no part of this book may be reproduced, or introduced into a
retrieval system, or transmitted, in any form, or by any
means (electronic, mechanical, photocopying, recording, or
otherwise) without written permission of the publisher and
copyright holder.

Printed in the United States of America

Some of the material in this book is new. Other updated
chapters originally appeared in a different form, some in
exactly the same form, in the books, *Wanted for Murder*
(Signet, ISBN: 0451169271), the *Dallas Observer*, and
Murderers Among Us (Signet, ISBN: 0451170571), and
online at Salon.com in 2000.

ISBN 1 92870422 0

Contents

Introduction

"You want know what's really interesting about homicide?" a veteran detective once asked us. "People actually have only a few different reasons for committing the crime, yet they keep inventing the most amazing new ways of doing it!"

His words came back to us as we were assembling Vengeful Heart. The would-be murderer of our title tale, for example, devised a unique and devilishly sophisticated way to commit his crime, and may yet succeed in it.

Throughout this collection, both the methods and the settings for homicide vividly underscore the investigator's point. The weapons range from a syringe to a woodchipper to a rock. The killings occurred in venues diverse as a moving vehicle in Florida, a pre-dug grave in Oklahoma and high in the Colorado Rockies, at thirty below zero, in the dead of night.

Whether you date the first-ever murder from the Book of Genesis (Question: What was Cain's weapon?), or to prehistory when a proto-human brute caved in a rival's skull (and, as recent archeological evidence suggests, may have proceeded to eat his victim) the crime has been deeply interwoven in our culture ever since.

Once it became illegal, murder quickly developed its own infrastructure. Judges, lawyers, investigators, jailers, jail builders, forensic scientists, psychiatrists, academics, reporters, photographers, artists, true crime writers, moviemakers and certain elected officials all in some degree owe their livelihood to killings, as well as to ancillary issues generated by these crimes. For instance, should society kill the killers, and if so, how?

Of course, the murder industry is predicated on the revulsion and fascination the rest of us feel toward homicide, a deep inner ambivalence reflected in our narrow and careful definition of the crime. We set the bar high. Taking another person's life is only the start. It must not have been a mistake or an act of madness. It must have no rational justification. To qualify as murderers—and thus for execution themselves —most killers must be sufficiently sane at the time of their crime to appreciate what they're doing. In other words, true psychotics need not apply.

A murder may be spontaneous, but it is always an act of volition. The killer knows he's doing wrong and can stop himself, but doesn't. Even then the ultimate penalty may not be applied unless prosecutors can also show the killing occurred in conjunction with another felony, such as kidnap.

Another homicide detective we know used to say that half the fun in any killing is trying to catch the guy (the other half was convicting and executing the guilty party). Every murder is a story as much as it is an act. Just as we cannot imagine a world indifferent to homicide, we can't cannot imagine a murder story that ends with the killing itself. True crime always has a beginning, a middle and an end.

This inherent narrative structure has attracted fiction writers to the subject of murder for millennia. From the Bible to Beowulf to Macbeth, murder occurs in our earliest and our grandest literature, and remains a central motif.

John Lanchester in his 1996 novel, *Debt to Pleasure*, even gives us a homicidal sociopath, Tarquin Winot, who exalts murder as the most refined modern expression of self, far more important than mere art.

"The artist's desire to leave a memento of himself is as directly comprehensible as a dog's action in urinating on a tree," the killer advises.

By contrast, a murderer "leaves behind something just as final and just as achieved—an absence."

Tarquin continues: "One must also face the sheer

naturalness of murder, the unnaturalness of art. Painting and music, books, they're so arbitrary, so over complicated, so full of invention and untruth compared to the simple human act of taking a life, because you don't want someone to carry on existing."

Tarquin Winot concludes with a query. "Who can deny," he wonders, "that murder is the defining act of our century, as other centuries might have been defined by prayer or mendicancy?"

Tarquin's a wee bit over-the-top. But what if your ruminator is a real serial killer?

We published two books about Ted Bundy, *The Only Living Witness* and *Conversation with a Killer*, both based on our extensive tape-recorded interviews with Bundy on Death Row in Florida. *Hollow Men*, the final selection here, draws on those long hours with Ted to address the concept Bundy first introduced to us—possession.

Ted said that for him possession was really the point of it all, to literally "own" a human body, "as one would possess a potted plant, a painting or a Porsche."

What a strange and alien notion, yet perfectly reasonable if you're a serial killer. It turns out that the absence of which Tarquin Winot speaks is actually the killer's empty interior, of which he is acutely aware. He does not create by erasure, because he is not an artist, but an abstraction, a hollow man, and he kills in a futile attempt to fill himself up.

To learn more, you're welcome within.

Stephen G. Michaud
Dallas
November 2000

The Vengeful Heart

The haunting of Janice Trahan began on the sultry Louisiana evening of August 4, 1994.

It was deep dark in Lafayette, the capital of Cajun country, about 70 miles southwest of Baton Rouge, and the thirty-four-year-old nurse was asleep, her three-year-old son, Jeffery, beside her in bed.

Then Trahan suddenly sensed a presence in the room. She looked up. By the dim light from the open bathroom door she saw Dr. Richard Schmidt, her estranged lover and the sleeping toddler's father, standing over them. He had a hypodermic needle in his hand.

Janice didn't immediately sense her peril. Although she just recently had severed a destructive ten-year relationship with Schmidt—they hadn't seen one another since July 19— this visit was not a surprise. Before their break-up, Richard had begun giving Janice B-12 injections he'd prescribed for her chronic fatigue. Tonight, he'd called to say he was coming over to give her another one. Janice even left the front door unlocked for him.

Yet the 46-year-old gastroenterologist seemed surprisingly nervous. Janice sleepily protested she'd decided against the shot—it was too late, she was tired—yet Schmidt ignored her, and proceeded with the injection before she could react.

There came a second surprise. Accustomed to the injections, Trahan knew what to expect. But this time there was searing pain as Richard squeezed the syringe's contents into her left arm. The fluid was the right color, light pink; but she never had experienced such agony from a B-12 injection.

No sooner was he finished than Dr. Schmidt hastily departed, explaining that he was needed in a nearby ER.

Later, when the throbbing in her arm did not subside, Janice paged him. At first Schmidt was angry, accusing his former lover of "checking up" on him. But when she explained her pain and confusion, the doctor softened. He promised, as she later told the court, "he wouldn't give me another injection in the dark."

He wouldn't need to.

Like any veteran detective, Lafayette police Capt. Jim Craft has seen a lot of behavior that is hard to understand, and much that is harder still to forget. But after nearly 20 years with the department, Craft had encountered nothing nearly so diabolic as the tale he heard in May of 1995 from district attorney Mike Harson.

The DA said a local nurse had come forth seeking a criminal action against a prominent Lafayette physician. As Harson told the story, Janice Trahan discovered in January that she was positive for both HIV, the virus that causes AIDS, and the hepatitis C virus, too. She accused Dr. Richard Schmidt of infecting her with both viruses via a hypodermic injection the preceding August.

The doctor's motive, she said, was revenge. Trahan explained how she had just terminated a ten-year affair with Schmidt. And his intent obviously was homicide; Janice Trahan knew she was a dead woman, talking.

It was a horrifying accusation. Who could wish anyone an excruciating death from AIDS, much less deliberately induce the disease? If the charge was a fabrication—as Capt. Craft at first suspected it was—an innocent physician's reputation, and career, possibly hung in the balance. If it was true, then Trahan had been the unsuspecting victim of a murder plot without precedent. No one ever had been charged and tried for attempted murder by HIV injection. It was a brand new way of killing someone.

Harson asked Craft to check out the nurse's story, and to

do so in the strictest confidence. At Lafayette PD, only Craft and his chief, Charles Crenshaw, knew of his assignment. Craft was forbidden even to tell his wife about it.

He began by interviewing Trahan, who told the detective that she met Schmidt in 1982 when she was a new hire at Lafayette General Medical Center. Janice was then twenty, married, and the mother of an infant son, named Justin. Richard, thirty-four and an ex-Marine, was married with three children. Two years later, after becoming Schmidt's patient, she also became his lover.

Trahan said she expected to start a new life with the doctor. She accordingly divorced her husband, just as Schmidt promised that he'd divorce his wife. But he never did. Instead, she told Craft, Richard strung her along for ten years. Over that time, he turned brutish, demanding and jealous. In July of 1994 she finally had enough, and broke off the relationship, she said. Two weeks later came the night of the mysterious injection.

Much of the story strained credulity with Craft.

"I didn't believe her," he says. "She had a 10-year relationship with this guy. Had a child with him. She said he came to her place one night and gave her a shot she didn't want, and she knew it felt different. Then she waited five months after learning she was HIV positive to come to the district attorney to request a criminal action be taken."

Craft took careful notes of his conversation with Janice Trahan. If she was lying, he knew, inconsistencies and con-tradictions would emerge. They always do.

However, it turned out that Janice Trahan had very plausible reasons for her delay in seeking out the DA. Initially, she told Craft, there was a strong desire not to have her appalling story publicly known. Secondly, Trahan had contacted a civil attorney soon after learning she was sick. It had taken some time for them to sort out her legal options. In the event, Mike Harson would ask Trahan to delay filing any civil action until Capt. Craft was well into his investigation.

Craft also was able to confirm other parts of Trahan's story. For example, she told him that she'd shared her concerns about the injection the very next morning with nurse Meredith Poche, with whom she worked in the intensive care unit at Lafayette General. Poche confirmed the story. Poche told Craft that Trahan said she suspected the injection Schmidt gave her was not B-12, and she wanted someone to know about the episode. Trahan told the same story to her supervisor, who also confirmed it to Craft.

"She also was able to pinpoint the date that the injection occurred," the detective recalls, "and she told us that he'd called her by cell phone to let her know he was coming over. We subpoenaed his cell phone records and sure enough, on August 4, 1994, there's a phone call to her house from his cell phone at 10:26 PM. Both the date and the time matched."

Craft now sensed there was substance to Trahan's allegations, but developing the proof to buttress them would not be simple. He assumed that the disease-tainted syringe no longer existed. Barring an unlikely confession from Dr. Schmidt, the only hope the police had was to somehow isolate the source of the infection. It was a long shot.

First, a search warrant was necessary. In order to secure it, Craft would have to convince a judge there was probable cause to believe Dr. Schmidt had tried to kill Janice Trahan. Just her story, including the parts Craft so far had been able to confirm, wouldn't do the job.

As it happened, Schmidt himself inadvertently supplied the added evidence. Following the injection, when Trahan developed troubling symptoms of HIV infection, Schmidt informed one of her doctors that he'd tested Trahan's blood, and that she was negative for the virus. That single lie, taken together with the rest of the evidence, was sufficient to secure Capt. Craft his search warrant.

On July 13, 1995, Craft deployed two search teams; one that he led to Dr. Schmidt's office, and a second group that went to the doctor's residence to prevent any possible destruction of evidence.

The search began after all of the doctor's patients and staff had departed, and the physician had called his attorney. After reading Schmidt his Miranda rights, the first thing Capt. Craft looked at was a large black binder—Schmidt's office appointment book. According to the detective, all entries for 1994 were missing.

When he was asked for Janice Trahan's medical records, Schmidt claimed he had none.

"She was my girlfriend, not my patient," Craft recalls the doctor saying.

"But as he said that he moved over and stood in front of the T section of his files. That was pretty obvious. We searched the T's and found a pretty thick medical file on Janice. There were tests and other things he'd done for ten years. Thus we knew right away that this guy wasn't going to be honest. He was going to lie to us."

Craft also asked Schmidt if he had personal items that Janice Trahan had given him.

"Look, I knew Janice," the doctor answered. "We had an off and on relationship for a couple of years and it was over. When we broke up I threw all that stuff away."

"I'm told you dated Trahan for ten years and you had a son with her," Craft calmly said.

Dr. Schmidt had little more to say during the rest of the search.

Capt. Craft had known next to nothing about AIDS, or how blood specimens are processed at medical facilities. But he quickly got up to speed.

"We found out," he says, "that you can't just walk into a hospital and steal a tube of blood that's contaminated with the AIDS virus. That's not the way the samples are marked.

"I learned that he most likely had taken the virus, and the hepatitis C, from one of his own patients. He then would have had to spin down the sample in a centrifuge to separate the plasma, which would have been light pink, just like a B-12 shot. So when we searched his office, we basically were interesting in finding out what patients he was seeing at the time, and whether we could trace the course of the infections through the records."

The investigators found Dr. Schmidt's centrifuge in his procedure room, where his staff took blood and prepared other tissue samples testing. Nearby were two spiral-bound notebooks, or "jot books," as Schmidt called them. One listed the names of all patients whose blood was drawn from March 1, 1993, to December 10, 1993. The second contained the same information from August 15, 1994, to July 13, 1995, the date of the search.

Inside the jot books, Craft noted that next to the patients' names and the dates their blood was drawn, handwritten notes indicated the type of blood tests to be performed.

Each entry also was accompanied by a little sticker with a code number on it. This, he knew, was called the accession sticker. Another sticker bearing the same reference number accompanied the specimen to the lab for tests. When the lab work came back, all the doctor's staff had to do was compare reference numbers to accession codes to match patients to their test results.

When Craft asked Schmidt for the jot book containing entries for December 11, 1993 to August 15, 1994, the doctor said he didn't know where it was.

Next, the team searched the doctor's personal office. "When we opened his desk, it was full of everything she'd ever given him," Craft reports. "Coffee mugs. Shirts. Cards and letters. Pictures of her. Pictures of their son. All of those things. We pulled all of it as evidence."

They also found a 1993 pocket calendar on top of Schmidt's desk. Inside were photocopies of sexually explicit photos of Janice Trahan.

There was a locked door behind Dr. Schmidt's desk. "What's back there?" Craft inquired.

"It's just a storeroom," said the doctor. "I keep old records and wine in there."

Craft opened the room and discovered that this time Dr. Schmidt was telling the truth. The storage room was filled with cases of wine that he gave away at holiday time as gifts to other physicians. There were several boxes of old records inside, as well.

By this time, Craft's team of crime-scene investigators had been working for two or three hours. They were getting "kind of cranky," as Craft puts it, and were ready to pack up and leave. However, Dr. Schmidt's blood still had not been drawn, and the captain intended to thoroughly search the storeroom, no matter how long that required.

"We'll probably have only one opportunity to do this," he told the rest of the team. "One shot." Unspoken was the fact that so far nothing they'd turned up was apt to convince a jury that Richard Schmidt had tried to kill Janice Trahan.

The storeroom search yielded nothing, either—until Craft was nearly done. He opened one of the few remaining boxes. There were records from 1982 on top. Deeper down, Craft found more ledgers and notebooks from the early '80s, nothing useful at all. But when the captain got to the very bottom of the box, he found a familiar-looking spiral-bound notebook, identical to the jot books next to the centrifuge.

Inside were entries dated December 14, 1994, to August 4, 1995, with several pages left blank at the end.

"I think you just found a smoking gun," a member of the search team remarked.

There were three names listed for August 4. Craft saw that two of the names had accession stickers next to them. The third did not. The only notation was "lavender stopper for Dr. S." written in a hand the investigator recognized as that of Dr. Schmidt's nurse.

By this stage in his serological studies, Capt. Craft had learned from an infection-control nurse at a Lafayette hospital that it is possible through so-called phylogenetic testing to determine whether a specific individual is the source of another person's AIDS infection. That is, there was a scientific way to show whether Janice Trahan was infected with HIV from one of Dr. Schmidt's patients.

The one patient who lacked an accession sticker for August 4, 1994, was a forty-year-old middle school teacher, Donald McClelland. Capt. Craft looked up McClelland in the Lafayette phone book, noted the address, and drove out to interview him.

After introducing himself at the front door, Craft asked, "Are you a patient of Dr. Richard Schmidt?"

"Yeah."

"Do you recall the last time you visited him?"

"I can tell you every time I've visited him," McClelland answered. "I've kept all my medical records."

"Would you check 1994?"

"When?"

"August."

"Sure." McClelland stepped away for a few minutes.

"Yeah," he said when he returned. "I was there on August fourth. But that wasn't a scheduled visit. I was called in."

Now came the payoff question.

"I think your blood may have been used for the wrong purpose," Craft said carefully. "I need to know something. Are you HIV positive?"

"HIV positive? I've got full-blown AIDS!"

Scientists at Baylor University College of Medicine in Houston required a full year to complete their phylogenetic studies in the case. In the meantime, Capt. Craft filled in the rest of Janice Trahan's story.

Her affair with Schmidt had begun with high hopes and great expectations.

"At first, everyone thought he was a good guy," Trahan's

brother-in-law, Elus Brasseaux, later told People magazine. "He was the perfect gentleman."

Schmidt even starting showing up for family dinner on Sundays. "He told us many times that he wanted a family with her, that he was definitely leaving his wife," added Trahan's sister, Becky Brasseaux. "But there was always an excuse."

"The evidence reveal[s] that sex was the primary focus when [Schmidt] and Trahan were together," a panel of appeals judges later would note, dryly. That certainly appeared to be true in Schmidt's case. Trahan described him as an urgently insistent, sometimes violent, lover. He refused to pull on a condom, and forbade her to use a diaphragm. Since Trahan could not tolerate the Pill—it gave her migraines—she inevitably and repeatedly became pregnant.

Three times, in August and December of 1988, and again in June of 1989, Schmidt convinced her to seek an abortion. Only once did he relent.

That was 1990. According to Janice, Richard had forced himself on her, impregnating her once again. But instead of once again insisting that she abort, Richard informed her parents, both staunch anti-abortionists, that their daughter was carrying his child. It was another way of controlling her.

The boy was born in 1991. Schmidt allowed their love child to have his middle name, Jeffery. But little Jeffery never would be a Schmidt.

As their affair turned increasingly rocky, Trahan was not without her means of retaliation. Under oath, she admitted to affairs with six other men during her ten years with Schmidt.

"Every time he wouldn't leave his wife, you'd start dating someone," a defense lawyer later observed to Trahan. "That got his attention, right?"

"Yes it did," she snapped back.

Trahan said the liaisons reflected her deepening

desperation to break away from the doctor. However, their most certain consequence was to provoke him.

Barry Bleichner, a Lafayette bachelor, met Trahan at a New Year's Eve party, and began dating her in early 1994. According to his later testimony, Bleichner invited Janice to a crawfish boil that spring. She accepted, then broke, the date, he said, explaining that Schmidt had grown furious when he learned they'd been seeing one another.

About a week later, Schmidt telephoned Bleichner. The doctor said he knew he'd been seeing Trahan, and recounted certain intimate details of the relationship, some of which were incorrect. Schmidt seemed to alternate between anger and calm during this conversation, Bleichner recalled. Before hanging up, the doctor also mentioned ominously that he knew where Bleichner lived.

A short while later, Schmidt telephoned once more, this time to apologize, and to ask that Barry not mention their conversation to Janice. It hardly mattered; Bleichner and Trahan no longer were seeing one another.

Dr. Schmidt was not finished, however. Bleichner was working in his front yard about a week later when Schmidt drove up and asked him for the return of some photos Janice had given Bleichner of herself. Bleichner replied that he'd be glad to return the pictures to Trahan, but not to Schmidt.

The doctor asked Bleichner if he'd like to fight, and told the younger man to take off his sunglasses. "He wanted to look me in the eye," Bleichner remembered.

Bleichner did not take Schmidt seriously.

"Richard, you're crazy," he said.

"Yes, I was trained that way," replied the Marine veteran. "If you see Janice again, I am going to kill you."

This was May, 1994. Trahan broke off with Schmidt two months later. Then came the mysterious injection. Within days of the shot, Janice developed persistent flu-like symptoms. On August 12, 1994, Richard ordered blood work done. According to Janice, he told her the tests showed that her white blood cell count was "a little low," but not to worry. She probably had a viral infection of some sort.

On August 16 Trahan visited her optometrist, Dr. Donner Mizelle. She complained that her throat was sore, and her lymph nodes were swollen. She was running a persistent fever. A pain had started up behind her eyes.

Thirteen days later, after suffering a two-day migraine, Trahan went to Dr. Robert Martinez, a neurologist who specialized in sleep disorders. She also complained of painful ulcers on her throat.

The ulcers, together with her swollen lymph nodes, were classic symptoms of a viral infection. So Dr. Martinez referred Janice Trahan to yet another physician, an ear-nose-and-throat specialist named Bradley Chastant. He saw Trahan immediately, and immediately ordered a lymph node biopsy, performed on September 16. The result indicated a so-called "viral reactive infection." However, a lymphoma —cancer of the lymph nodes—couldn't be ruled out.

Chastant referred Trahan to Dr. Luis Mesa, an oncologist, or cancer specialist, who first examined her in his office that day, September 16. However, before seeing Janice, Mesa called her former lover to discuss her condition.

Dr. Mesa would testify that Dr. Schmidt said he suspected Janice suffered from an unspecified viral infection, although it couldn't be HIV. She'd already tested negative for that. As a consequence, Dr. Mesa did not order his own HIV test, noting on Trahan's chart that she'd already tested negative.

Janice Trahan's symptoms would not go away. On November 12, she visited her dentist, Dr. Neil Bernard. He noted that her gums were inflamed, her lymph nodes were swollen and her white blood count was elevated.

Finally, on December 15, Trahan went to her OB-GYN, Dr. Wayne Daigle, for her annual check-up. Like every other doctor before him, Daigle suspected a viral infection. Unlike the others, he ordered a battery of lab work that included the HIV test. Five days later, the awful news came back: She was HIV positive.

Daigle waited for the Christmas holidays to be over before delivering what was tantamount to a death sentence. Five months after the fact, a stunned Janice Trahan finally understood what actually had occurred that night in early August. In all likelihood, Richard had murdered her.

Trahan asked Dr. Daigle to contact Schmidt, whose office was downstairs from the OB-GYN's. The two physicians met at the building's back door. Daigle testified that Schmidt seemed shocked to learn that Trahan was HIV positive. Since Daigle was aware of their ten-year relationship, he presumed that Schmidt was HIV positive, too. Schmidt, however, insisted that he was not infected, that he felt fine, and that he did not need to be tested.

In a telephone conversation later that evening, Daigle offered to have Schmidt tested anonymously. Schmidt again declined, and suggested that Trahan may have contracted AIDS in a variety of ways that had nothing to do with him. He specially mentioned her contact with AIDS patients at the hospital, her other sexual partners and her possible exposure to HIV during her three abortions.

Daigle didn't believe any of it, and informed Schmidt he was duty-bound to tell the Louisiana State Board of Medical Examiners that Schmidt was potentially HIV positive.

In mid-1996, the Baylor researchers finally reached their conclusion: The genetic material from Donald McClelland and Janice Trahan was "closely related." At trial, another expert, Prof. David Hillis of the University of Texas Institute of Molecular and Cell Biology, would call the two viral strains "as closely related as sequences from two individuals could be."

On Tuesday, July 23, 1996, a Lafayette grand jury formally charged Dr. Schmidt with second-degree attempted murder. Janice Trahan was not specifically identified in the indictment. Reporters wouldn't learn her name until a judge unsealed Trahan's civil suit.

Still, the media had no luck reaching her for comment. "She is a victim and she is fighting her battle for survival," Trahan's attorney, James R. Leonard, declared in a written statement. "She is not interested in publicity, and only hopes for a fair and speedy trial."

Public reaction to the indictment was mixed. In the medical community, Dr. Schmidt's colleagues, most of whom were well aware of the affair for years, tended to side with the doctor. Nurses, however, rallied to Trahan. Dr. Schmidt was not popular among them. Some were openly derisive about Dr. Schmidt's "comb-over" haircut. Others used "creep" to describe Schmidt to reporters.

There certainly was no consensus about the doctor's guilt or innocence around the city of Lafayette. "People don't know which side to believe," Jim Bradshaw, the metropolitan editor for the Lafayette Daily Advertiser told Russell Miller, a British writer. "I think everybody is just leaning back and thinking, 'My God, what is the world coming to now?'"

Schmidt's local attorney, Frank Dawkins, of course insisted to the press that his client was innocent. Dawkins even intimated that Schmidt had an alibi defense.

The doctor said nothing while he remained in jail. But the week following his Friday, July 26, 1996, bond hearing, where Schmidt posted $500,000 and was released, he took out an ad in the Advertiser.

Under the headline "A NOTE OF THANKS," Dr. Schmidt thanked "all of the patients and friends that (sic) have called or written to voice their support over the past week." He described the charges against him as "totally untrue," and denounced unspecified "statements made to the media" as "untrue or distortions of the truth, made in an obvious attempt to discredit me which is both irresponsible and unconscionable."

He concluded, "Rather than being critical of my attackers, I wish that you would pray for them and forgive them. The path of forgiveness is not the easy way, but it is the right way. We will however continue to fight this injustice with all means possible."

Richard J. Schmidt, MD

His public indignation and high-mindedness notwithstanding, Dr. Schmidt did have some explaining to do. Capt. Craft's surveillance over the past year turned up a new love interest in his life, his nurse Alice Bryan. Long before the relationship was discussed at trial, Ms. Bryan moved to Pennsylvania.

Schmidt's attorneys also raised the fact that Donald McClelland did not suffer from hepatitis C, seemingly undercutting the possibility that McClelland was the source of Janice Trahan's AIDS infection. In response, Capt. Craft re-examined the spiral notebook he'd recovered from the storage room, and saw that on August 2 a second patient's name was entered without an accession sticker. The only notation was "Purple Top for Dr."

Her name was Leslie Louviere. She told Craft that Dr. Schmidt had treated her for hepatitis C. For insurance reasons, Louviere went on, her blood always was drawn at Our Lady of Lourdes Regional Hospital. However, she remembered that on August 2, 1994, a blood sample had been drawn at Dr. Schmidt's office. Louviere remembered that the doctor explained he needed the specimen for a research project.

The State of Louisiana versus Richard J. Schmidt went to trial on Thursday, October 15, 1998.

"It was a tough case," says assistant district attorney

Keith A. Stutes, the lead prosecutor, "because it was a totally circumstantial case. The scientific evidence didn't prove he did it, or not. It really boiled down to the rest of that evidence."

That meant a conviction would require Richard Schmidt's jury believe Janice Trahan and the circumstantial evidence against the defendant. Or 10 of the 12 jurors had to. In Louisiana, in non-capital cases, at least 10 jurors' votes are required either to convict, or to acquit a defendant. Otherwise, the jury is hung and a mistrial must be declared.

It is yet another feature of Louisiana law that the prosecution's burden of proof is slightly different when the evidence is substantially circumstantial (as opposed to physical, such as a fingerprint, or eyewitness). Rather than needing to establish guilt "beyond a reasonable doubt," the prosecution in circumstantial evidence cases "must exclude every reasonable hypothesis of innocence."

In Janice Trahan's case, that meant narrowing the possible sources of her double viral infections to Richard Schmidt.

On Day One of the trial, under questioning by Stutes, Trahan told her story for the first time in public. After she described how Schmidt repeated promised to leave his wife, Barbara, and then didn't, Stutes observed, "This sounds like old news by now. Why did you continue this relationship? Why didn't you just break it off?"

"I ask myself that all the time," Trahan answered. "I was weak. There were threats. I didn't have control over my own life."

According to Trahan, Schmidt said he'd kill her and himself if she ever left him. He also threatened to post his erotic photos of her around the hospital, or to inform the University of Southwestern Louisiana, where she'd taken her nursing degree, that he'd helped her cheat on her course work.

When her love for Schmidt finally was overwhelmed by

the barrage of lies and intimidations, said Trahan, she decided to leave him. She claimed even to have asked for Barbara Schmidt's help in extricating herself from Richard. When at last she did, a final warning from him kept ringing in her mind.

"If you leave me," he told her, "I'll drive you to suicide, and I'll make sure that no man will want you."

"She was a very good witness," says prosecutor Stutes. "She was genuine, credible. She was honest. She bared her soul, which is not easy for any witness. And she was subjected to brutal cross examination."

Part of Trahan's ordeal was the necessity of identifying in court every man with whom she'd had sex since 1984. There were seven of them. Stutes then introduced serological evidence that all seven, including Schmidt and Trahan's new husband, Jerry Allen, were HIV negative.

Keith Stutes then attacked his second hurdle, excluding every other reasonable hypothesis. The fact that she was a regular blood donor eliminated the possibility that she'd contracted HIV during one of her abortions. She'd given blood in April of 1994, long after her last abortion with Schmidt, and had been negative for both HIV and hepatitis C at the time.

Dr. Ernest Wong, a Lafayette pulmonologist who specialized in AIDS treatment, also testified that based upon his long experience with the virus and its symptoms, he believed Trahan was infected during the first week of August 1994.

Schmidt helped out the prosecution, too. By bringing up the fact that Trahan was doubly infected soon after his indictment, he unintentionally drew the noose of circumstance even tighter around his own neck. Where else might Janice have contracted both viruses?

The defense did offer two proactive arguments for Schmidt's innocence. One was that he'd been home the night of August 4, and in his wife's company. Barbara Schmidt testified that Richard was only out of her presence for the twenty minutes she spent taking a bath. This was insufficient time, the defense argued, for Schmidt to drive the five miles to Janice Trahan's apartment, inject her, and return home before his wife completed her bath.

However, a Lafayette police officer made the circuit twice in under 20 minutes, both times observing all traffic laws.

Schmidt's attorneys also argued that he'd suffered a back strain lifting luggage at a seminar in late July 1994. The pain and stiffness, they said, would have slowed him considerably, making such a 20-minute circuit to Trahan's apartment from his house a practical impossibility.

Maybe so, but when he'd visited his doctor about the condition in early September, 1994, Schmidt specifically mentioned that he'd reaggravated the injury lifting boxes at his office in August. Mrs. Schmidt testified to a similar conversation with her husband.

"We note," the appeals judges later wrote, "that the lifting of heavy boxes by Defendant in his office in 1994 is consistent with the State's theory that he hid the jot book containing the August 4, 1994, notations at the bottom of a stack of file storage boxes in his office."

His trial lasted eight days. At 8:35 PM on Friday, October 23, 1998, after taking 10 votes, the nine-woman, three-man jury came back with a 10-2 guilty verdict.

"I believe justice was served," juror Roy Ellis later told reporter Bruce Schultz of The Advocate. "I believe he's a very disturbed individual. He destroyed many lives, including his own."

According to news reports, Janice Trahan cried as she heard the verdict and then fainted. She was taken from the courtroom in a wheelchair. Barbara Schmidt broke into tears as well, and stood with her husband as he comforted her long after the jury had departed.

Dr. Schmidt remained free on his $500,000 bond until

sentencing in February of 1999. He did not testify at his trial, but at the sentencing hearing he characterized himself as a victim in the case, arguing that Janice Trahan had manipulated him. Nevertheless, he added, "I feel a great deal of compassion for Janice and her family."

At the close of the hearing, District Judge Durwood Conque sentenced Dr. Schmidt to 50 years at hard labor, the stiffest penalty possible. "In the final analysis, the punishment must fit the crime," said the judge.

Janice Trahan again was in court that day, and again had no public comment.

Since then, Richard Schmidt has vigorously pursued his appeals on various grounds. In the summer of 2000, his attorney Herbert Larson argued before Louisiana's 3rd Circuit Court of Appeal that the state had tried to prove his client guilty "by character assassination." The panel upheld Schmidt's conviction late in July of 2000.

His victim's medical outlook is uncertain, but in an ironical way remains a topic of paramount concern to Schmidt. Under the doctrine of double jeopardy, a defendant can only be tried once for a criminal act. So if Janice Trahan were to die from her viral infections, Dr. Schmidt could not be retried for her murder.

However, if Dr. Schmidt's appeal succeeds, his case would be remanded to the original court in Lafayette, where prosecutors will have the option of re-indicting and re-trying him. If in the meantime Janice Trahan does die from AIDS or Hepatitis C, then the DA will be free to consider homicide charges.

Richard Schmidt must be careful what he wishes for.

Up in Flames

Houston oil mogul Edward Gerald Baker was known as an intelligent opportunist, a man who played both sides against the middle—a man who buoyed himself up from near-poverty to become one of the Bayou City's fastest-moving, most noticeable and best known promoters.

Baker, 52, always seemed to have an entourage with him —young executives, hopeful to get close to some of Baker's legendary oil deals; beautiful women, hopeful they might become one of Baker's "chosen."

But no matter how many times the local newspapers chronicled Baker's successful strikes, innovative dealings and "reorganizations," there always remained an intriguing "underside" to Baker's swashbuckling facade.

Whether it was the rumor mill, that insisted Baker was making his millions at the expense of others, or the law suits that questioned his veracity, Baker's reputation and Horatio Alger-like aura seemed on the decline in 1985.

Most people close to Baker were predicting the high-living oilman's bubble was bound to burst soon. But, these same folks would tell you in the next sentence, "Ed will figure out a way to end up owning the town and smelling the roses, no matter what."

Baker's car, a sleek 1984 Jaguar, was found burned out one Friday morning in November of 1985 in a rice field near Katy, Texas, just a few miles west of Houston. Inside the still-smoldering automobile, about 30 pounds of charred bones and other human debris lay on the seat and floor.

Nearby was a .32 Smith & Wesson revolver, known to be Baker's.

The early morning discovery was big news in Houston,

where nearly everybody had heard of Baker or had crossed paths with him at some point.

There seemed to be more theories than facts—right from the outset.

Immediately, speculation built that since there was physically so little left of the body, "Fast Eddie" Baker might have faked his death and taken off for his beloved Caribbean, to live out his years in luxury instead of battling contentious legal suits and what he told friends was an almost sure divorce, which he thought would leave him financially strapped.

A Houston private detective, Bob Gale, said he would bet "everything I have" that Baker had set up the situation to fool authorities into thinking he had been burned to death.

"He is an intelligent man," said Gale, who had handled many, many private eye assignments for Baker. "He's living it up somewhere far from Houston. I never felt anything else," he said.

"Well, it's either one of the most clever suicides or one of the most clever murders ever," said Harris County sheriff's captain Mike Smith at the time of the discovery.

One less than friendly business associate put it this way to Kathryn Casey, who wrote of the strange case for *Houston City Magazine*: "Edward Baker was an entrepreneur living the 'American Dream'—and then he screwed the family pooch. If he didn't die in a ball of flame in his '84 Jaguar, he died in the flame of his own greed."

One round had been fired from the .32. A shotgun was also in the back seat, as well as three fire-damaged gasoline cans which authorities figured contained the fuel used to torch the Jaguar.

Baker's wedding ring was found fused to the metal of the auto's chassis, an indication of the intensity of the fire; another ring was virtually unharmed.

As law enforcement officials cordoned off the site from the gathering crowds, they made another startling discovery.

Less than a quarter mile from the fire scene, they tumbled across the body of a young man, thought to be in his mid-20s, manacled and very dead, lying in high grass. He was clad in nothing with a T-shirt and had been beaten to death.

Though police intensified the search for this victim's killer, thinking it must have been somehow related to the Baker homicide, they never found him or her. Indeed, they never even identified the body. They doggedly ran his fingerprints through all the usual databases to no avail.

Meanwhile, one of the nation's most noted medical examiners, Harris County's Joe Jachimczsk, was trying to make some sense out of the charred remains found in the Baker car.

He found that while it was a certainty that the body had been cremated inside the car, he could not say decisively that the fire was a direct cause of death. The situation was further fuzzied, Jachimzcsk said, by the fact that Ed Baker had suffered from advanced coronary arterial sclerosis, meaning that if the body inside the car *had* been Baker's, he could have suffered and died from an infarct.

That was the medical examiner's gut reaction early on. At first he identified the remains as Baker based on a few dentures. Investigators pointed out that Baker's wife had told them that Baker had a duplicate set of dentures. They wondered if he might have tossed that second set in the car to help make his case.

Later on—though it did not completely satisfy the cops —Jachimczsk said he had strengthened his "call" from additional jawbone fragments, which he matched with Baker's dental x-rays. Likewise with the victim's palate, the medical examiner contended.

Jachimczsk said it was one of his toughest autopsies ever.

"The big handicap," he explained, "is that we didn't have enough of him left. There was a gunshot wound to the head. But we don't know whether it was self-inflicted or not."

Finally the medical examiner said he figured it was suicide, but said the victim might have had "some assistance."

"We can't rule out a homicide," said Ronnie Phillips, a detective with the Harris County sheriff's office, one of six different agencies that investigated the Baker case.

Terry Wilson, then a Harris County assistant district attorney, harbored many doubts about the situation. He leans away from the suicide theory.

While he tentatively accepted that the remains were those of Baker, "I never ruled out the possibility that it was somebody else in that car."

Subsequent tests, he explained, "pretty much indicated that Baker could not have shot himself and ignited the gasoline."

But, unless a snitch comes forth, he admits, authorities may never know what *really* happened. "I would guess that until some crook runs his mouth off," he said, "we won't solve the case."

Baker was considered nice looking, a man who constantly worked on his appearance.

Private eye Gale said Baker had had at least two facelifts. An ex-partner, Bob Busey, said Baker was vain. "On a scale of one to ten, I'd say he was a 13," said Busey, who added, "I never saw him pass a mirror without glancing, or stopping to straighten something."

He was usually driven around town in a stretch limousine and was seen at high-level social events, clad in expensive clothing, occasionally a top hat.

"I know of times when he drove up to the front of a gala, and got out when he wasn't even going to the function," said the ex-friend, Busey. "He knew the photographers were there."

Baker often told stories of intrigue, including one tale that he had Mafia connections.

This fabrication in time blossomed into yet another

theory of his demise. Sandra Baker, his fourth wife and widow, would speculate that Miami mobsters might have murdered her husband.

Baker did have unsavory associations. Police sources say blackmailers once threatened him. The details of the case are unknown, but as one cop put it, "I think he tried to cheat the wrong people. Sometimes when one hustler gets hustled by another, all Hell breaks loose."

Bob Gale helped Ed Baker out of the blackmail, but also refused to discuss the matter. Gale's more open about the females in Baker's life. While an earnest womanizer, Ed Baker nevertheless was "uncomfortable" with his women, says Gale. He often instructed the investigator to follow them. Gale recalls shadowing various wives and girlfriends to "Florida, New York, California—all over."

The oilman also routinely asked that his employees at Vanguard be surveiled. One term for such obsessive distrust is paranoia.

Baker's first wife, Sally, whom he married in 1953, died in a 1973 car accident. His second marriage, to Marie Ella Walker, ended in divorce. Karen Wallbridge was his third wife. He met her at a meeting of EST guru Werner Erhard's often-lampooned human potential training program.

Baker married Wallbridge in Las Vegas in September of 1984. Less than two weeks later, he filed for an annulment, claiming he was drunk during the wedding ceremony. On April Fool's Day, 1985, Baker and Wallbridge were divorced. A month later, and just seven months before his Jag was discovered aflame, Baker married Sandra, who had been his secretary.

Ed Baker started out as a traveling shoe salesman, then moved to insurance and real estate sales before discovering his forte—the oil-drilling business or, more exacting, the oil drilling promotion business. Along the way, he met the famous wildcatter, Glenn McCarthy, and helped McCarthy launch his novelty whiskey, Old Wildcatter.

Through his Vanguard Groups International, Inc., Baker formed tax-advantaged partnerships for wealthy Texas drillers who wanted to elude and evade as much federal tax as they could. For a while, business was good and many well-known Texans got richer, along with Baker.

Typically it would be 12 to 24 partners, investing like amounts to drill dozens of wells.

"For the investor with tax problems, this was a honey of a deal," one of his former partners told the *Houston City Magazine* reporter in 1985. "Baker was getting the reputation of a man who delivered," he added.

Some say it was the lure of Las Vegas that eventually did Baker in. Others say his lifestyle was more expensive than his earning. But whatever the reason, along in 1984 or thereabouts Baker began shoveling money his partners intended for drilling into his private coffers. Within months the syndicate business was suffering and several of his partners got together to check the books.

That led to the first of several civil suits. And soon it was discovered that Baker owed three Las Vegas casinos about $50,000 each. He told his wife, according to her, that he borrowed money from the Miami mob to pay off these Las Vegas debts—thus the rumors that persisted after his death.

"A lot of men who get into financial trouble try anything to make the big hit," said private detective Gale. "That's the reason he gave me for his gambling. He had a lot of faith he would hit it big."

Baker's lawyer, Ward Busey, said he thought the stories of his client's heavy gambling were overplayed. Busey also does not believe Baker killed himself. "Ed never gave me any indication he even contemplated suicide," said Busey.

But he *did* tell Busey, the lawyer claims, that he was being threatened and was fearful for his life.

Just days before his death Baker rewrote his will by hand, allocating $500,000 for his new wife Sandra and splitting $600,000 between three children. Busey received the new wills in the mail the day after Baker died.

The only person who talked of Baker's plan for suicide was Sandra. She told the cops he talked incessantly about killing himself in the days just prior to his death and even checked to see how much insurance he had.

She also pushed forth the idea that mobsters might have killed because of the half million he allegedly owed them.

Clyde Wilson, 77, just retired as Houston's best-known and most successful private detective, said recently the rumors about the mob doing away with Baker were "bull-crap."

"It was a hit and I think everybody pretty much believes now that the job was hired by his wife," Wilson said.

Wilson, who had been hired by Sandra Baker shortly after Baker's death, said in later years he had disproved the mob allegation.

"I met with the 'man from Miami,'" said Wilson, who said that Mrs. Baker had told him about Baker's fears that "they were ready to come kill him." He said Baker owed the mobster only $15,000, hardly enough to have somebody killed.

Wilson said he began to distrust Sandra Baker from the first time she came to his office to hire him.

"She told me that Ed had told her to pack up all her jewelry and get out of town, out of harm's way," said Wilson.

Wilson asked her why, once she was out of town, expecting that her husband's life was in danger, she didn't call the police.

"I didn't want to get involved," Wilson said she replied.

Five days after the body was found, and at Clyde Wilson's insistence, Sandra Baker took a polygraph at the Wilson detective agency offices.

She was asked if she knew who had arranged her husband's death, if she had participated and if she was withholding any information about her husband's death.

Sandra Baker replied "no" to all three questions but examiner Bob Musser detected she was not being entirely forthcoming.

"We thought she was trying to hide something," said Musser. "It looked deceptive in nature," he told a reporter.

Later his report said:

"Her physiological responses are in such a pattern to cause the examiner to believe that she is in fact withholding information concerning the death of Ed Baker."

Told that she had been taking tranquilizers, Wilson suggested she return for a second test a few days later.

"She said she would, but I didn't really think she would," said Wilson. "When she came back at the appointed time, she refused and I asked her to leave the office. That was the end of it."

Five insurance companies were involved. Three reportedly paid the widow more than $300,000; the other two balked, one complaining that it would not pay because it was a suicide, the other refusing to acknowledge that Baker is dead.

Reprinted from *Murderers Among Us*

"It Has to Be Family"

The decrepit three-story apartment house at 5635 Clemens in the Cabanne (pronounced Cabiny) neighborhood of St. Louis, Missouri, was at one time a proud structure and a very respectable address. By the early 1980s, however, Cabanne was in steep decline and the sturdy brick residence had become an abandoned, derelict shell. The upstairs floors were forlorn and drafty. Below ground, the aged building's capacious basement storage alcoves—one for each apartment—stood silent, dark and dank as tombs.

On February 28, 1983, a cold and clear Monday, James Brooks, a 29-year-old self-employed auto mechanic, and Gregory Edwards, 23, who was then unemployed, were out scavenging in the vicinity of the dilapidated apartment house. Brooks' car had broken down about a block away and the two men were looking for a piece of scrap metal to serve as a bar, or lever, to help fix the vehicle's drive train.

When they got to the alley behind 5635 Clemens, Brooks and Edwards saw a row of concrete steps leading to the building's basement door. They decided to follow them.

According to former Detective Sgt. Joseph Burgoon of the St. Louis metropolitan police department, the underground complex that Brooks and Edwards were about to explore was pitch black and eerie. "It was like catacombs down there," he says. The only light source was Brooks' disposable cigarette lighter, which he flicked on and off as they gingerly felt their way through the storage rooms.

The friends inspected two alcoves and found nothing of use. Then they moved on to a third area, which turned out to be the boiler room. In the dark, James Brooks again flicked his lighter, then froze in horror at what it revealed. There on the floor in front of him was a headless human form, clothed only in a yellow sweater.

"They came flying out of there real fast and called the police," reports Burgoon.

He and the four other homicide detectives on his shift were notified of Brooks' discovery at 3:45 PM. When the detectives arrived at the scene, the house already had been sealed off by uniformed officers. Fire department personnel were stringing electric lights in the basement.

In the boiler room, the detectives had discovered that the prone, headless victim was a black female. Her hands were tied behind her back with a length of red-and-white nylon rope. Jane Doe was very slender, and in life stood about five feet three inches tall.

"We didn't know what we had at the time," says Burgoon. "We thought she might be a prostitute or something."

Not until an autopsy was performed did the police learn that Jane Doe was no hooker, but a healthy, adequately nourished, prepubescent child between the ages of 8 and 11. The medical examiner said the little girl had been raped. Cause of death was manual strangulation.

By the look of her neck wound, and the striations on her exposed vertebrae, the girl's head had been sawed off with a large blade, possibly a butcher's knife. There were no other physical signs of injury or abuse.

There was almost no blood in her body, which suggested the girl had been killed elsewhere, and later brought to the boiler room. Traces of her blood were discovered on the basement walls. Apparently her severed neck had brushed the walls as the killer carried her body down into the boiler room.

A fungus was growing on her neck, which gave the detectives a way of inferring how long the little girl had lain on the boiler room floor. A specimen of the fungus was taken to the Missouri Botanical Gardens in St. Louis, where it was cultivated under the same temperature, humidity and light conditions of the boiler room. It required five days for the fungus to grow, indicating that probably was how long the girl had lain undiscovered.

"It was just a freak thing that Brooks and Edwards stumbled in there and found her," observed Burgoon. "Otherwise she probably would have been in there a long time and all that would have been found was her skeleton."

The girl's yellow sweater didn't tell them much. The Orlon garment was fairly new, well made, and it fit her. The label had been cut out, pointing to the possibility that the sweater was purchased at the type of discount store where the names of well-known manufacturers or designers are removed from sale items. No leads ever evolved from this supposition.

The police at first thought it would be a relatively simple matter to identify the victim. "We assumed she was from somewhere nearby," says Leroy J. Adkins, who was a captain in command of the homicide squad at the time. "We also assumed she had relatives, neighbors, friends, or schoolmates who would report her missing," Instead, as Adkins puts it, "This has been one of the most perplexing cases I have ever seen."

It seemed likely that the killer was a local man, or at least he was familiar with the neighborhood; no stranger was apt to know about the abandoned basement, much less would he have taken the dead girl back three rooms to dispose of her. Similarly, he must have brought Jane Doe to the house on Clemens St. at night. No one careful enough to hide her as he did would likely risk being seen with her body, and perhaps recognized, in the daytime.

Unfortunately, their reasonable assumptions brought detectives no closer to apprehending Jane Doe's killer, nor did they establish her identity. Absent any witnesses to the crime, or report of a missing child that fit Jane Doe's description, the police took their investigation to local schools.

"We figured this child had to be in school somewhere," says Joe Burgoon. "Right away we checked the schools in the neighborhood there real close, thinking she might have been from the neighborhood or a housing project two blocks north. Nothing. No one fitting her description."

Next, the police went to the St. Louis Board of Education where they secured a complete record of transfers and withdrawals among St. Louis city schoolchildren. Unfortunately, recent school budget cuts had eliminated follow-up record keeping. Once a student withdrew or transferred, no one double-checked to see if he or she actually re-enrolled. Within the previous 12 months, more than 600 young African-American schoolgirls in St. Louis had been withdrawn from their schools, or were listed as transfers.

Detectives Burgoon and Wayne Bender personally tracked down each and every one of them.

Still no leads.

The search then was expanded into surrounding St. Louis County. Approximately 150 names emerged and, once again, Burgoon and Bender checked out all of them. "That was a lot of tedious work," says Burgoon.

Some of the girls, mostly from military families, had moved as far away as Europe. When the list had been pared down to a handful for whom there was no trace whatsoever, the police arranged for their names and descriptions to be aired on local television. Viewers were able to account for every one of them.

By contrast, the detectives' search for missing black girls through the vast slums of East St. Louis, across the Mississippi River in Illinois, went nowhere. "Some East St. Louis schools sent us their records," Burgoon recalls. "Others didn't. We talked to social workers and explained to them what our problem was. They said it was just too monumental for them. Parents come in and apply for aid, but they never see these kids, unfortunately."

Nationally, the case was sent by teletype to police

agencies in all 50 states. Her story has been distributed, as well, to every missing-child registry. In the spring of 1991, Burgoon even told Jane Doe's story to a national television audience on Oprah.

The case has been entered into VICAP, the FBI's computer database of unsolved murders. The Bureau would have profiled Jane Doe's killer, too, says Burgoon, but too little is known about the victim and the crime for the FBI's experts to provide their behavioral insights.

In yet another measure designed to make the Jane Doe murder as well known as possible, Leroy Adkins personally contacted every U.S. periodical with a significant black audience, asking each paper and magazine and journal to publish a description of the case. "I've never seen an investigation as intense, as exhaustive, as this one," says Adkins. "We've done everything we can do."

At one time, the detectives also had what seemed to be a good suspect, possibly Doe's biological father. He was brought to their attention by a female acquaintance who reported that she had seen the man with a little girl in a yellow sweater about a week before James Brooks and Gregory Edwards discovered Jane Doe's remains.

Subsequent investigation revealed that this individual once had been arrested for menacing people with a large knife in a St. Louis city park. The suspect told arresting officers that he was an undercover Secret Service agent.

Unfortunately, DNA tests eliminated him as a suspect.

Detectives have interviewed a child killer on death row in Missouri in connection with the case. And most recently they have taken an interest in Tommy Lynn Sells, a drifter who has confessed to a dozen murders in seven states, dating back to the 1980s. Now on death row in Texas for 1999 throat-slash murder of 13-year-old Kaylene Harris in the border city of Del Rio, Sells has said he's committed similar murders across the country, including one in St. Louis.

The strongest possibility in Jane Doe's case, however, is

that the little girl was killed by a close relative, and that members of her family have guilty knowledge of the crime. Perhaps she was from an East St. Louis household. And perhaps neighbors and friends were given some story to explain her sudden disappearance in 1983. The police can only hope that someday one of these acquaintances might come forth with the break they desperately need to solve the terrible crime.

"It has to be family," says Leroy Adkins. "It has to be. And I would say they lived right here. When we identify her, we'll probably know who killed her."

Reprinted from *Murderers Among Us*

Mom and Dad

When reporters talked to William Leslie Arnold's teachers at Central High School in Omaha, Nebraska, they were told that the sixteen-year-old junior was a quiet, well-behaved boy who played the clarinet and tenor saxophone, did fairly well in class and was rarely absent.

Others, however, knew Leslie as a willful juvenile delinquent, "a high-strung, flighty boy," according to his uncle Ben McCammon, and a terror to the other kids in the middle-class neighborhood where he was raised. One local adolescent told the Lincoln (Nebraska) *Journal* that Leslie was feared for his violent temper, and that with very slight provocation he recently had tried to throttle this youth's younger brother.

This was in the autumn of 1958, and the reason that the Nebraska press was so curious about William Leslie Arnold was that the boy had just been charged with murdering both his parents.

The killings occurred in the late afternoon of September 27, a Saturday. As Leslie later explained in his confession, his mother, forty-year-old Opel Arnold, had caught him in an untruth about three weeks earlier, and as punishment had forbade Leslie access to the family car. Leslie also had been in trouble with his parents for monopolizing the family telephone with calls to his girlfriend, Christine, whom Leslie was determined to take to the drive-in movie that Saturday night.

These are the surface facts of the case. Leslie, a jug-eared kid with the nervous habit of chewing on his lip, may also have been abused by his parents. Decades later, a relative would assert that parental abuse at least partly explained what was about to occur.

When Opel still adamantly refused to let Leslie use the car that night, the boy went upstairs and came back down with a .22 semi-automatic rifle. He squeezed six shots into his mom's heart as she stood in her dining room.

His dad, William Arnold, forty-two, came home a short time later and discovered Mrs. Arnold dead on the floor. According to his son, Mr. Arnold tried to grab him but missed, and then Leslie shot his dad, too, six times in the chest.

He wrapped his parents' blood-soaked corpses in an eight-by-ten rug and dragged them down into the basement. Back upstairs, he mopped up the remainder of their blood with two of Mrs. Arnold's small throw rugs. These he later tossed into a nearby creek, along with the larger rug.

The teenager next took a shower and changed his clothes. Then Leslie climbed in the family car and drove into the huge Ak-Sar-Ben (that's Nebraska spelled backward) racetrack across the street, where his younger brother Jimmie worked as an usher. Leslie told Jimmie that their parents had decided on the spur of the moment to go visit relatives in Loup City, Nebraska, a small town on the Middle Loup River in Sherman County, about 150 miles due west of Omaha. While Mr. and Mrs. Arnold were away, Leslie said, Jimmie was to stay with uncle Ben's family, which Leslie already had arranged. He drove Jimmie over to uncle Ben's that evening, then picked up Christine for their date at the drive-in.

The next morning, Leslie borrowed a neighbor's shovel, explaining that his parents wanted him to do some work in the garden while they were away. That night, with brother Jimmie conveniently removed to uncle Ben's house, his big brother carried William and Opel up from the basement and buried them under three feet of soil in their backyard flower bed, near the lilac bush.

Leslie's story of mom and dad's sudden departure for

Loup City stood up for a few days. Then neighbors and relatives, including Ben McCammon, began to wonder what was going on. Calls to Loup City established that the Arnolds had not arrived there, nor had they been expected. A missing persons report was filed with the Omaha police.

A week later, the boy's paternal grandparents drove to Omaha from their house in North Loup (northeast of Loup City). They, too, stayed with Ben McCammon and his family, while Leslie continued on alone at home.

By this time, uncle Ben and the other relatives harbored dark fears of foul play, and some family members had a suspect in mind. They noted that Leslie was conducting himself with uncommon civility ever since his parents vanished. That made Ben McCammon especially suspicious.

On Friday night, October 11, thirteen days after William and Opel Arnold last were seen alive, McCammon called a family council to be held at the Arnold house. Leslie skipped the meeting for a high school football game that night.

"We felt we'd waited long enough," McCammon explained to the Omaha *World Tribune*. "Mrs. Arnold [Leslie and Jimmie's grandmother] didn't want to call in the police. The rest of the family kind of overpowered her. It's lucky we did."

In the midst of these discussions, Leslie Arnold came home from the football game. His aunts and uncles told him what they intended to do. According to McCammon, "he seemed totally unconcerned."

On Saturday morning, October 11, the police put Leslie through a more focused interrogation than they had before, and this time the teenager confessed what he had done. Leslie took investigators to his parents' improvised graves in the flower garden, and stood by impassively as first Opel, and then William, was exhumed. Mrs. Arnold's feet were bound with a leather belt. Leslie's only outward sign of emotion at the exhumation came when a neighbor cried in disbelief, "Oh, Leslie! How could you do it?"

His lower lip quivered.

Leslie was stonily aloof at his arraignment, and did not betray any emotion as he was charged with two counts of first-degree murder, to which he pleaded innocent.

After spending eight months in the county jail, Arnold accepted a plea bargain. In exchange for a guilty plea, the charges were reduced to second-degree murder, and he was sentenced to two lifetimes in the Nebraska State Penitentiary.

Eight years later, on July 15, 1967, Leslie Arnold broke out of the state prison with another murderer, thirty-two-year-old James Harding. The pair cut through the steel bars in a hobby-room window. Sometime after six o'clock that night, they slipped through the window and up over a twelve-foot fence to freedom.

The next day a motorist reported seeing two men clad in prison-issue and answering to Arnold and Harding's descriptions prowling around a farm machinery shed near the town of Pickell, thirty-two miles southeast of Lincoln.

Eighty cops and prison employees descended on the rugged, swampy countryside. They combed it, inch by inch, under a brutal sun. Great clouds of mosquitoes rose up from the fetid creek bottoms to bite them. The search went on for two days before authorities gave up in despair. Prison warden Maurice Sigler called the escape "one of the cleanest getaways" in his experience.

The following year, James Harding was recaptured in Los Angeles. Nebraska law enforcement officials have had no such luck with Leslie Arnold, who has successfully eluded them now for more than thirty-three years.

In 1999, an individual identifying himself (or herself) only as Leslie Arnold's cousin posted a plea on *www. unsolvedmysteries.com* for the 57-year-old fugitive to give himself up. Changes in the abuse laws, the writer said, made it possible that if Leslie turned himself in he might only have to serve the portion of his sentence stemming from his escape.

Leslie Arnold so far has not accepted the invitation.

"Seems to me you might want to leave him alone," suggested another writer in response to the posting.

"Maybe he doesn't want to be found," said another.

"He might not even be in the United States," offered a third. "He could be your next door neighbor in disguise. Ever think of that?"

Reprinted from *Wanted for Murder*

Suspect

Is Jeffrey Oberholtzer of Alma, Colorado, indeed the anguished widower he claims to be, still mourning his murdered wife Bobbie, and angry that authorities still have not identified her brutal killer, let alone arrest him? Or, as his younger brother Jamie suspects, is Jeff Oberholtzer himself the killer—a double killer—and an amazingly durable dissembler who so far has not betrayed a trace of guilt for the merciless crimes he committed on a bitter cold Epiphany Night, January 6, 1982?

"I can't prove it," says Jamie Oberholtzer. "All the evidence is what you call circumstantial. But I do believe he killed her."

Jeff responds that his brother may be blinded by his own unrequited love for Bobbie. "She was a very lovable gal," he says. "He had a crush on her, and I married her. I love my brother dearly, but he's messed up my life real bad."

Here are the background and details of the bloody night, together with the puzzling, contradictory evidence that tends both to implicate Jeffrey Oberholtzer, and to exonerate him in the gunshot murders of his wife and another female of his acquaintance, 21-year-old Annette Kay Schnee:

Barbara Jo Burns was born on Christmas Day, 1952. She spent her girlhood in Racine, Wisconsin, where she matured into a spirited young woman, about five feet three inches tall, 110 pounds, with blue eyes and blond hair. Bobbie became pregnant while still in high school, and left before graduation in order to have her baby girl, whom she named Jackie. She subsequently married the child's father. They were amicably divorced in 1974.

That same year, Bobbie, then 22, moved to the Mt. Snow

region of southern Vermont with another Racine youth, 19-year-old Jeff Oberholtzer. They returned to Wisconsin and married there in 1978. Bobbie's ex-husband meanwhile took custody of Jackie.

Jeff worked as a machinist, fabricating garbage disposal systems in the local In-Sink-Erator plant, while he learned home appliance repair from Bobbie's father. After belatedly completing high school, Bobbie was employed as a waitress, a chambermaid and as a clerk in a Racine pet store. She loved animals.

In May of 1980, after several visits to Colorado, the couple decided to quit their native northern plains for a new life up in the Rockies. They settled in Alma, an old mining town on State Route 9, below the Continental Divide and steep Hoosier Pass from Breckenridge, the more affluent vacation ski village 17 miles to the north.

Jeff Oberholtzer opened a repair business, "Alpine Appliances," which he operated out of their rented duplex in Alma, right on Route 9. Bobbie took a secretarial job at a local real estate firm, and also bartended part-time at Alma's Only Bar, also known as the A-O-B. In January of 1981, she landed a more lucrative position at Cal-Colorado, a real estate investment company up Route 9 and over Hoosier Pass in Breckenridge.

Their combined incomes allowed the Oberholtzers to just get by, week by week. Yet though they were chronically short of cash, they did manage to buy Bobbie a horse, a $75 mustang she called Nakoosa, and to make a down payment on a potential homesite, a two-acre lot in neighboring Park County. Jeff secured the loan for the land with his Ford pickup and a coin collection.

Brother Jamie Oberholtzer, who followed Jeff out to Alma from Racine, alleges that there were significant strains in the Oberholtzer marriage, problems stemming in part from Jeff's drug use. Jamie's wife, Cindy, whom he met and married in Colorado, makes the same argument. Although

Jeff concedes that he did consume controlled substances, he insists that his marriage to Bobbie was solid. According to Richard Eaton, who at the time was an investigator for the local Summit County sheriff's department, police inquiries turned up no inordinate problems in the Oberholtzer marriage.

Jeff wrote poetry. Bobbie raised birds; finches and a cedar waxwing she'd discovered injured in Wisconsin and nursed to health.

Sometimes they fought. On Monday night, January 4, 1982, for example, Bobbie was supposed to come home with a hot pizza for dinner. She was late. The pizza was cold. Jeff lost his temper. Jamie claims Jeff was so irate that he took a swing at Bobbie, missed, and put his fist through a wall.

The argument spilled over into the next day and evening at a bar and, later, was duly recounted by witnesses to the police. "The cops just blew it all out of proportion at the time," says Jeff. "We have a fight over cold pizza, and so I murdered her?"

Another point of contention: Jeff says Bobbie was ready to have another child, and that she stopped taking her birth-control pills on January 2, 1982. Jamie and Cindy deny this was so. They insist that later they found a note in the Oberholtzer residence—unsigned and undated but clearly in Bobbie's hand—which read, in their paraphrase, "If you kill me today, how can I ever have your child tomorrow? You don't know what I just found out."

Jamie and Cindy say that the note was handed over to the police, and probably what Bobbie had "just found out" was another instance of philandering: They accuse Jeff of chronic womanizing. Investigator Richard Eaton said he never saw the note, and has no knowledge of the alleged message.

The last day of Bobbie Oberholtzer's life, January 6, a Wednesday, began as most weekdays did with a 5:30 alarm. According to Jeff, Bobbie readied herself for work as usual, then asked if he had a little money to help buy some golden raisins; her finicky waxwing would eat nothing else. Oberholtzer scrounged up his last few quarters for her.

Since Jeff needed the Ford pickup for his business, Bobbie was obliged to hitchhike to work, which she did not particularly relish. However reasonable that point of view was, Bobbie's husband insists the practice was common in their group at the time, and that hitching in the Brackenridge area was not particularly inconvenient, or dangerous, even for a young woman. Bobbie never rode with a stranger. "You stood out at a certain spot in front of the house or in Breckenridge," he says, "and people who knew you would pull right over. You didn't have to stick your thumb out. It was like a community carpool-bus stop."

A cup of coffee in hand, Oberholtzer watched from a window that morning as his wife stood in front of their duplex, waiting for a lift. He remembers seeing a car stop for her, and that he didn't recognize the vehicle, which carried out-of-state plates. Whoever the driver was, he or she delivered Bobbie safely to work at the Cal-Colorado offices on time at 8:30. She spent an uneventful day at her desk.

Annette Kay Schnee of Blue River, Colorado, on the north side of Hoosier Pass, was a willowy native Iowan, and inch or two taller than Bobbie Oberholtzer. She weighed just 95 pounds. Her eyes were brown, as was her hair, which Annette streaked with a blond rinse. According to her mother, Eileen Franklin, Annette was a member of her high school drill team in Sioux City, and later studied modeling in Omaha. Before moving to the Breckenridge area, where she had many friends, Annette often talked of becoming an airline stewardess.

In contrast to the assertive and high-spirited Bobbie Oberholtzer (with whom she may have had a nodding familiarity), Annette Kay Schnee was docile and given to moods. In her diary, she often complained that life was unfulfilling, that men seemed to take her for granted. "I feel I need to get my act together here real soon," she wrote on January 2. "I'm not sure what's in store for me... this year. But it should be real interesting."

At 3:30 on the frigid, clear afternoon of January 6, Annette Schnee finished her shift as a chambermaid at the Holiday Inn in the town of Frisco, about ten miles north of Breckenridge along Route 9. She had about five hours off before she was scheduled for work at her second job, waitressing cocktails at a Breckenridge nightspot known as The Flipside.

Like Bobbie, Annette hitched almost everywhere she went. Her first stop that afternoon was the Summit County Medical Center, also in Frisco, where she was treated for a yeast infection. Next, Annette headed south down Route 9 for Breckenridge and a pharmacy, The Drugstore, where she would get her prescription filled. A local man later told police he drove Schnee halfway to Breckenridge. How she made it the next five miles is not known.

Pharmacist Bob Beitcher remembered filling her prescription. Annette walked out The Drugstore door at around 4:30. Beitcher's only other relevant recollection was of another white female, unfamiliar to him, who seemed to be with Annette that afternoon. She was dark-headed, probably in her early twenties, about five-three, with a medium build. Schnee reminded her companion that she needed cigarettes. "Oh yeah," the woman answered, and bought a pack of Marlboros. She has never been identified.

Annette's next destination was a house she shared with five other single people about a half-mile off Route 9 in Blue River, another small mountain community, six miles south of Breckenridge. She was due home to change into her night uniform, the cowboy hat and hotpants Annette wore at the Flipside.

She never made it.

Full darkness descended over Breckenridge by late

afternoon on the sixth. With the sun gone, the ambient temperature plummeted toward its overnight low of around 30 below zero. People bundled themselves in several layers of clothing wherever they went.

At a little past five, according to Detective Eaton, Bobbie Oberholtzer called home to tell Jeff that she was going to have a drink with friends at a bar called The Pub in the Bell Tower Mall, a short walk from the Cal-Colorado offices. There was no answer down in Alma.

At 6:20, Bobbie called Jeff again from a pay phone at The Pub. This time he answered. According to Jeff Oberholtzer, he and his wife discussed what they would eat for dinner—pot roast, probably—and Bobbie informed him that her friends, Char McKesson and Dan Carey, would be driving her home.

An hour passed. "Supposedly," says Detective Eaton, "she started getting upset with these people because they didn't want to go home. She told the bartender that she was going to call home. She grabbed some change and went into the hall and came back a few minutes later, grabbed her coat, and told the bartender, 'I'm gonna leave. Don't tell them I've gone for a while. Just tell them I'm going to hitchhike home, thanks anyway.' Then she left."

According to this version of events, Bobbie had a short walk to a convenience-store parking lot where she and other hitchhikers customarily waited for rides south on Route 9 over Hoosier Pass to Alma. At approximately 7:50 that night, a local resident stopped his truck at the store and offered a ride to a hitchhiker who fit Bobbie's description; the man even accurately described the clothes Bobbie wore that day. He told investigators that she declined to get into his truck because he wasn't going all the way south to Alma. This man was the last person to report seeing Bobbie Oberholtzer alive.

Jeff Oberholtzer disputes both the bartender and the truck driver. He says he told his wife by telephone that if she wanted a ride she need only call home. "I told her, 'If you want me to come get you, I'll come get you.' She said, 'Don't worry about it. I'll see you when I get home.'

"I believe that she walked back to the telephones and saw someone she knew and they went out the door together. That's why she didn't go back in the bar. It was 30 below that night, with the wind blowing. There was no way she was going to go outside and hitchhike home when she could have made a telephone call to me."

Down at their rented house in Alma, Jeff seems to have received a steady stream of visitors that afternoon. After questioning them all and double-checking their stories, Detective Eaton does not believe Jeff Oberholtzer could have been away from the Alma residence for more than a couple minutes from around four or four-thirty until some time after six. Telephone company records support Jeff's memory of answering Bobbie's 6:20 call from The Pub. Still later visitors to his house place Jeff there, watching television, at least until eight.

Alone in the house, as he explained to investigators, Oberholtzer put away the uneaten dinner—including the chocolate pudding he'd made for dessert—and continued watching television. He grew increasingly upset with his wife for not coming home, or even calling.

He dressed for bed, and was able to sleep, he says, until 12:10 A.M. when Oberholtzer was startled awake by a police or ambulance siren, wailing south on Route 9 toward the town of Fairplay, six miles away. Jeff says he dressed and moved to the couch, where he dropped off again, until approximately 2:10 A.M.

It was too late to call The Pub, so Jeff jumped in his pickup and drove over to his brother Jamie's house. "He was having a screaming fit," Jamie recalls. "'Bobbie's dead! Bobbie's dead!' And I said, 'What are you talking about?'

"'Oh, she's dead! She's not home. If she was alive she'd be home! She's dead!'" Jamie Oberholtzer also remembers that his brother was freshly showered, which to him seemed odd considering the hour and circumstance.

Jeff, who's last quarter had gone for raisins that morning, borrowed $5 from Jamie and then headed out to Char McKesson and Dan Carey's house. He awakened them, and asked what they knew about his missing wife. His friends explained that Bobbie had consumed about three rum-and-Cokes with them. Their only other information had come from the bartender, Gus Garbounoff, who told Char and Dan that Bobbie departed on her own at about 7:30 to hitch a ride home.

"Again," Oberholtzer insists, "that didn't make sense to me. She knew I was at home. The thing that sticks in my craw is that *no* locals hitchhiked over to Alma at that time of night, especially in that kind of weather."

Jeff drove north to the Cal-Colorado office in Breckenridge where, he says, he jumped up on the garbage dumpsters so he could peer down into Bobbie's office. He remembers thinking that she may have drunk too much at The Pub and, for some reason, returned to her desk and dozed off.

There was no sign of Bobbie, however, and all Jeff got the several times he dialed her office number was Bobbie's recorded voice. "Afterward it was eerie, thinking about that," he recalls.

Oberholtzer's next stop was the Breckenridge police department, where he reported his wife missing. It was now about 3:30 A.M. According to Jeff, he spent the balance of the night driving around the area, searching for Bobbie.

By nine o'clock that morning, he had returned home where he received a call from rancher Donald Hamilton of Como, a little community 10 or 11 miles northeast of Fairplay on Route 285, the main road to Denver.

Hamilton reported that he had just found Bobbie's driver's license in his yard. Subsequent searches of the area revealed that the license together with the rest of contents of

Bobbie's wallet apparently had been flung onto Hamilton's property, probably from a moving vehicle on Route 285. The wallet itself was not recovered.

Jeff dispatched Jamie to retrieve the license, and then joined friends as they searched Routes 9 and 285 between Alma and Como. About four miles southwest of Como they found Bobbie's distinctive blue backpack along the side of the road. Nearby, they recovered one of her gloves and a wadded up tissue. Both were stained with human blood, type unknown. A Kool filter cigarette butt lay there, too.

Some hours later, a snowplow operator working the east side of Route between Alma and Fairplay 9 came upon her leather cosmetic pouch. It was resting on a roadside snow bank.

The various discoveries of Bobbie's personal belongings along the local roadsides suggested that someone had driven south in the night along Route 9 to Fairplay, and then northeast on 285 toward Denver, tossing her things out of the car as he drove. On the other hand, this might have been a deliberate deception, a red herring designed to lead the investigation away from the killer.

Actually, the official investigation had yet to start. Jeff and his friends took Bobbie's belongings to the sheriff's office in Fairplay, and once again reported her missing. But the sheriff made no immediate move to join the hunt for Mrs. Oberholtzer. In fact, a deputy suggested to Jeff that Bobbie may simply have left him. That was the usual explanation in most such missing person cases.

As it happened, the question of Bobbie Oberholtzer's fate would be quickly resolved.

At three o'clock on the afternoon of the seventh, fewer than 20 hours after she was last seen alive, a party of searchers on skis discovered Bobbie Oberholtzer's frozen corpse. She had taken two bullets, and was lying in deep snow at the top of Hoosier Pass, about 65 feet west of the Route 9 centerline. She was fully clothed.

The authorities pieced together this probably scenario for Bobbie Oberholtzer's final minutes and murder.

She was so adamant about never hitching with strangers that unless the multiple rum-and-Cokes had unduly affected her judgment, it seemed likely either that Bobbie knew her killer, or that she was coerced into his vehicle, perhaps at gunpoint.

A nylon wire restraint, similar to the plastic "flex cuffs" that some police departments use in place of metal hand-cuffs, was attached to her left wrist. This was an important clue. Bobbie Oberholtzer's killer came prepared for his work; he was no novice.

The restraint was looped through a second wire, clearly meant for her right wrist.

If her attacker's intent was rape, he had been foiled. The coroner reported that Bobbie had not been sexually violated. Instead, judging from the bullet wounds and blood and footprint patterns at the crime scene, it appears that she broke loose from him in the parking lot and took off, running south along the crest of Hoosier Pass on Route 9, toward home.

She made it about 100 yards. Bobbie then must have clambered to her right up the roadside snow bank where she turned around, perhaps to plead for her life. He shot her, twice. One bullet grazed her right breast. The other slug, the fatal one, pierced her right lung.

Blood spatters and her footprints preserved in the otherwise undisturbed snow suggested that she tumbled down the other side of the snow bank, away from her attacker, who did not try to follow her. Mortally wounded, Bobbie stumbled on through the snow until she hit deep drifts, then willed herself back north along the snow bank, rapidly losing strength. Her scarlet trail then veered wildly to the west (had he shot at her again?) away from the road, to a point where she collapsed and bled to death.

One day later, on January 8, one of Annette Schnee's coworkers at the Holiday Inn in Frisco reported her missing to the Summit County sheriff.

Early on, there was reason to believe the two cases were connected. An orange footie of the sort Annette Schnee was known to wear over her knee socks was discovered on Hoosier Pass, about 100 yards from where Bobbie Oberholtzer was found. That could not have been a coincidence.

Still, no appreciable investigative progress was made in either homicide until the following summer. In the late morning of July 3, 1982, vacationer Arthur S. Davison of Denver called the Park County sheriff to report that his 13-year-old son, Allen, had just discovered a dead woman lying facedown in Sacramento Creek.

Annette Kay Schnee had been found.

The first fact of interest was the location of her body. To reach the creek site, Annette's killer had turned west off Route 9 into County Road 14, about a mile and a half north of Fairplay. He then drove about three miles to a spot just short of where County Road 14 ended in a cul-de-sac barely wide enough for an average-sized vehicle to make a U-turn.

County Road 14 was little more than a gravel track. Most motorists along Route 9 wouldn't even notice the turnoff, especially at night. Therefore, it was the near-universal assumption among investigators who worked the Schnee murder case that her killer knew beforehand about County Road 14. They were looking for someone local.

Important clues also emerged at Annette's autopsy; some of them forensic, others inferential. Her body was far too decomposed for the medical examiner to establish whether she'd been sexually assaulted. However, as Schnee's clothing was being removed, one of her knee socks (which she wore over her long underwear) was discovered stuffed in her sweatshirt pocket.

This was a strong clue. According to her mother, Annette

was a meticulous dresser, unlikely ever to have any article of clothing, no matter how insignificant, out of place. Since she'd clothed herself after her visit to the doctor on the afternoon of January 6, the most obvious explanation for the displaced sock was that she'd disrobed and then redressed herself under extreme stress.

None of her clothing was torn or otherwise damaged, and her body bore no signs of a physical struggle. Her single injury was a 1/4-inch wide gunshot wound in her back. The firearm was of unknown caliber, not dissimilar from the weapon used to kill Bobbie Oberholtzer. Like Bobbie, Annette's right lung had been perforated by the bullet. She also probably bled to death.

The motive for killing either victim is a matter of speculation. Perhaps they knew their attacker. Annette Schnee probably jumped or was pushed from his vehicle and, again much like Bobbie, was fleeing on foot through the deep snow for her life when he shot her in the back and left her to die.

There have been no arrests made in either the Oberholtzer or the Schnee murder case, nor have authorities focused on any suspects except for Jeff Oberholtzer.

It made sense, at first, to key on Oberholtzer. If the crimes were connected, as everyone believed, and if the killer was an area resident, again as most people thought, then a third factor also cast the shadow of suspicion over him.

The majority of murder victims know or recognize their killers. Jeff Oberholtzer's business card was found in Annette Schnee's ski jacket pocket. He created further problems for himself by initially denying that he knew the woman. Only after Schnee's picture appeared in the local paper did Oberholtzer remember that he'd once given her a ride.

His greatest difficulty was the total lack of other good suspects. Jeff claims he was harassed, unremittingly, The police, he says, would show up to ask questions even when he was out working on customers' appliances in their homes. Business soon dried up, and he later turned to plumbing. Similarly, he alleges, the police would contact and question any female he saw.

"I lost friends," Oberholtzer explains. "This has blown a lot of good things for me. It's all been downhill."

Even after he volunteered for, and passed, both a polygraph and a hypnotic exam, Oberholtzer remained a prime suspect.

"On paper, he is the most logical suspect," says James Hardtke, a former investigator with the Colorado Bureau of Investigation, who worked the two murders. "In reality, I don't think he did it. And if he did, he planned it really well. He's psyched himself into thinking he didn't do it, or that it was totally justified."

Then there are Jamie and Cindy who firmly subscribe to Jeff's guilt, even if their proof is (literally) insubstantive. They speak of a spectral being known as Mr. Death, or sometimes Mr. Darkness.

After Bobbie's murder, Jeff moved to a new house which, he says, harbored an evil spirit that sat at night at the end of his bed. The being also revealed itself one night to Cindy as she slept in the house with Jamie.

"It's not occult," she explains. "It's just karma. I just happen to see spirits. I always have. Whenever they come around they usually come over and say, 'hi.'"

The night in question came at least a year after Bobbie's murder. Cindy recalls having a dream shattered. "It was like a hammer hit it," she says. "Like glass. I jolted up and faced the doorway to his bedroom and this thing just sort of materialized. It was huge, black, very dense, like a cloud. Really dense. It was about seven feet tall. I figure it woke me up coming after me, and I just stared it down. I knew it wanted Jamie. But I stayed up all night, staring it down. As soon as dawn hit, it just dissipated, right?"

Cindy Oberholtzer believes the apparition was a spirit of vengeance out to find justice for the slain Bobbie Oberholtzer. Jeff argues that Mr. Death was a site-specific spook—he only saw the thing while he lived in the house, which he long since has left—and it might be some mournful old mountain miner lost between heaven and hell. He vehemently denies that Mr. Death had anything to do with guilt for his wife's murder, or the suicides Jeff has occasionally contemplated in his darker moods since the crimes.

Detective Eaton, who says he has heard all of Cindy and Jamie's allegations, can't see what they add up to. "There's a lot of supposition and theory," he says. "There's nothing in there based on fact."

After many years of thinking otherwise, Eaton came to agree with Jim Hardtke that Jeff Oberholtzer really is as innocent as he insists. "We've pretty well eliminated him," says Eaton.

Unfortunately, moving suspicion away form Oberholtzer has not necessarily been accompanied by a movement of suspicion *toward* anyone else—although Jeff himself has suggested that maybe his younger brother merits consideration.

A new task force—involving several counties in the area—has for months been looking into what its leader term "new evidence and new witnesses" and expects to add knowledge, if not indictments, to the strange case.

Reprinted from *Murders Among Us*

Camacho

For agent Tase Bailey, the transforming moment came as they unearthed the victims, dumped together in their rural grave. The FBI man had seen many dead bodies before, but never a bullet-riddled mother and her little boy, curled up in his pajamas, murdered for no reason at all.

Suddenly, what began as a routine drug case no longer was.

Bailey vowed to track down their killer and did, by luck and guile, artfully luring him into a trap. Now, on a summer evening 10 years later, the agent would keep a second promise, to watch the infamous Genaro "Geno" Ruiz Camacho—among the most feared and despised defendants ever tried in a Texas courtroom—die by lethal injection.

Standing silently in the low-lit cool of the death chamber's witness room, he stared at the doomed man who was strapped to a gurney, an intravenous line sticking out of his arm. Executions ordinarily didn't interest Bailey, but Camacho was no ordinary criminal, and the white-knuckle struggle to catch him—a secret operation until now—had been no ordinary investigation. Bailey still was haunted by what he'd discovered at Camacho's crime scenes: In a brief spasm of violence, the fugitive had taught the FBI agent and other North Texas investigators more than any of them cared to know about the darkest side of human behavior.

Bailey also knew another unnerving thing about the coolly self-contained, even genial, prisoner, who now was chatting amiably through the window with his family. Camacho very nearly eluded capture altogether.

Without a serendipitous assist from an unexpected source, plus exceptional luck and the success of a clever subterfuge, he never would have been brought to justice.

Imagining that possibility was another good cause for Bailey to wish Camacho dead. His loathing for the killer was palpable, a bitter knot inside him. And now that Camacho's legal ammunition was spent, Bailey was free to express it.

"Suck it up, Mr. Badass," he muttered beneath his breath. "You're going to be dead in about five minutes."

The chemicals began to flow, and Bailey could hear the killer's family in the adjacent room, banging at the glass, hoping for one last glance from their dying husband and father. It didn't come.

Then the prison doctor stepped forward to pronounce Camacho dead, and Bailey finally pulled his gaze away from the lifeless figure. Geno Camacho was dead. Bailey turned, and as he walked out into the warm Texas night he felt the hard lump of hatred begin to dissolve.

FBI violent crimes squads are do-all teams responsible for everything from chasing down federal fugitives to catching bank robbers. In the spring of 1988, besides their normal caseloads of maybe 30 investigations apiece, Bailey and his 13 fellow agents on the Dallas FBI's violent crimes squad were busy with the heart-breaking, unsolved, abduction-murders of two girls, as well as the recent capture of a notorious serial bank robber, known locally as the Dapper Bandit.

Then, around 8:30 on Friday morning, May 20, four male UNSUBs—unknown subjects in FBI parlance—burst into a crack house in the southeast Dallas neighborhood of Pleasant Grove, where the intruders abducted Evellyn Banks, 31, a sometime drug dealer, and Banks' 3 ½-year-old son Andre. Witnesses said two of the kidnappers appeared to be Hispanic. The third man was Anglo and the fourth black.

Sam Junior Wright, 52, Andre's father (and a fugitive drug dealer himself), had run from the house, shouting to neighbors to call 911. When the Dallas police arrived, they discovered the body of 25-year-old David Wilburn, Sam Wright's nephew, slumped on the floor. A single .357 slug had been discharged at close range into the back of Wilburn's head.

Though bloody and violent, the episode was unexceptional in the illegal drug trade, what some jaded narcs call a "misdemeanor homicide." Agent Bailey, who had taken Friday off to be with his oldest daughter as she had her tonsils removed, heard about the incident on the radio, and paid the news no special mind. Then early the next evening, Bailey received a telephone call at home from agent Jose Figueroa, also of the violent crimes squad.

Figueroa explained that Sam Wright, now in hiding, had telephoned the FBI to report that the leader of the kidnap gang was an Hispanic drug dealer known to him only as "Geno," who had snatched Evellyn and Andre as hostages against $30,000 Banks owed him for 25 pounds of marijuana. David Wilburn, Wright continued, was an innocent victim. The volatile Geno had grabbed an accomplice's handgun, pushed the mildly retarded Wilburn to the floor and executed him—simply to underscore how serious he was about recovering his money. Wright's only other information was that police in Mesquite recently had arrested Geno.

Agents Bailey and Figueroa recognized one fact for a certainty. Geno's extremely poor impulse control did not bode well for Evellyn and Andre Banks.

If mother and child were to survive, the FBI would need to act swiftly. The odds weren't good in any case.

"Can you help me tomorrow?" Figueroa asked.

"I'll see you in the morning," Bailey replied.

His first stop that Sunday was the Mesquite police department, where detective Capt. Larry Sprague told Bailey that Mesquite police indeed had recently arrested 33-year-old Genaro Ruiz Camacho. The stocky, swarthy suspect—5'-7",

175 pounds—had been detained in March on a hot-check warrant. But a routine records check had revealed something far more ominous. Camacho was a fugitive from the South Texas hamlet of Mercedes, his hometown, where the previous summer he had shotgunned a man to death over a trivial, name-calling dispute. Following his arrest in Mesquite, Camacho was held briefly at the Lew Sterrett Justice Center in Dallas before being returned to Mercedes, where he posted a $35,000 bond—in cash—and was set free to await trial.

Bailey also learned from Sprague that Camacho was well known as a mid-level player in the Dallas illegal drug market. He was said to have a cold, Mephistophelean stare, with which he controlled his frightened wife, Vickie, and also scared the hell out of several lawyers Vickie had hired in abortive divorce proceedings against him.

Although the investigation hardly had begun, a consistent and deeply troubling psychological profile of Geno Camacho was beginning to form in Bailey's mind. The dope-dealer-turned-killer already was known to have needlessly murdered two people. How long would such a killer be likely to keep Evellyn and Andre alive?

Capt. Sprague provided Bailey a mug shot, a rap sheet, and an address for Vickie, who then lived in Mesquite with her kids.

"Vickie told us a lot about Geno's background," Bailey recalls. "How abusive he was. She hadn't seen him in a month or two, but said she was scared of him and wanted him off the streets."

Vickie Camacho also helped Bailey find Wanda Jackson, her husband's girlfriend, who lived in Garland. Jackson, an attractive black woman who wore special contact lenses that turned her eyes blue, was an expensive dresser, Bailey recalls, and a very evasive interview subject. No, she hadn't seen Geno since they'd attended a family funeral on Thursday. No, she had no idea where he was.

Bailey would later learn from a member of Camacho's gang that Jackson in fact had just returned from spending the weekend with Camacho at a Dallas hotel. "Your big brother has been here," she telephoned her boyfriend as soon as the FBI agents left, "and he says you are a bad boy."

Late that Sunday, May 22, the violent crimes squad regrouped at the FBI's Dallas offices. The assembled agents quickly surmised that the black male reported with Camacho at the crack house crime scene was Wanda Jackson's 24-year-old brother, Juan, who became the second object of the investigation.

Also on Sunday, capital murder and kidnapping charges were filed against Camacho. A press release, along with Camacho's mug shot, was provided to *The Dallas Morning News*.

The paper's story on Monday prompted a local bartender to report Geno Camacho had been in the club where she worked on the previous Thursday night.

He'd been in an angry and threatening mood, she said, and had been in the company of a good-looking, muscular male in his twenties, whom the bartender knew only by the nickname Fast Eddie.

Another caller, a David Munoz in Fort Worth, claimed that he knew Geno Camacho from the drug trade. In a secret meeting held at an Arlington motel near Six Flags, Munoz told agents Bailey and Sherman Hopkins he believed Camacho's unidentified white male accomplice was likely one of three people. Munoz's first two suggestions didn't pan out. His third guess, Eddie Blaine Cummings of Lawton, Oklahoma, was a bull's-eye.

Fast Eddie was a precocious felon. Only 24, he already had committed a lengthy list of offenses from narcotics violations to illegal weapons possession to stealing several thousand dollars from his mother. Jail records also indicated that Cummings had been Geno Camacho's cellmate at the Sterrett Justice Center for a few days earlier that spring, while Camacho awaited his removal back to Mercedes.

A check with Cummings' parole officer revealed that Cummings' last known address was a two-bedroom apartment in North Dallas. The apartment now was empty, and Fast Eddie was missing. A federal parole violation warrant was issued for Cummings.

Within hours of identifying Cummings, the FBI also heard again from Sam Junior Wright. Realizing they needed the frightened Wright if they hoped to rescue Evellyn Banks and Andre via a potential ransom deal, agent Figueroa came up with a scheme to capture him. On the phone, Figueroa told the fugitive drug dealer he was leaving the office, and asked Wright to call back at another number in 20 minutes. In the meantime, 10 two-man squads of agents were deployed in unmarked cars around Wright's known South Dallas haunts, and a trace was set up on the phone.

When Wright called again, Figueroa kept him talking long enough for his location, an Oak Cliff convenience store pay phone, to be established. Agents rushed to the address, but then allowed Wright to drive away, under close surveillance. When they were certain Camacho's gang wasn't also watching Wright, the pulled him over and arrested him.

The plan was to use Sam Wright to lure the kidnappers into the open with the bait of a $30,000 ransom. Wright, who was headed back to prison on drug charges one way or the other, was willing to cooperate. But even though Camacho had told Wright that $30,000 would buy back Evellyn and Andre, unharmed, and had given him a cell phone number to call when he had raised the money, the number never answered. By the end of the week, the possibility of ransoming the Bankses seemed dead.

It is axiomatic in law enforcement that for each day a case remains open the odds against successfully closing the file lengthen dramatically.

Although the FBI quickly had identified their suspect, as

well as two of his three accomplices, by the end of the first week the trail was cold.

"There was lots of frustration," Bailey says. "We had no idea where Camacho was, or what he'd done with his hostages. He made no effort to contact anyone about a ransom. All that we knew about Cummings was that he'd left town. Juan Jackson had vanished too. We didn't know if they were together, or apart, or what."

In fact, no substantive new leads surfaced until mid-June, when a local topless dancer named Pamela Miller was reported missing. A friend told police that Miller, 23, who danced at a joint near Bachman Lake called Baby Dolls, recently had told her that she'd witnessed "something she shouldn't have" and that she would be going away for a while. Another friend recognized Camacho in the newspaper as the man she'd seen in company with Miller and others at Baby Dolls.

June turned to July with still no progress and scant remaining hope that Evellyn and Andre Banks were still alive. Then came the first of two lucky breaks. In early August 1988, about 10 weeks after the kidnapping and murder in Pleasant Grove, a snitch reported to the FBI that the fugitive Eddie Blaine Cummings was hiding out in Lawton, his hometown, and planned to be at a certain restaurant there on a certain day.

Federal marshals were on hand to spoil the meal.

August 7, agents Figueroa and Christopher Lawlor interviewed Cummings in the Lawton jail. He confirmed what they'd already surmised: Geno Camacho had recruited him into his drug organization while they were cellmates at Lew Sterrett. Cummings also disclosed that the missing Pamela Miller had been his girlfriend.

Early on the morning of May 20, he told the agents, Camacho had appeared with Juan Jackson at the North Dallas apartment Cummings shared George David Cooke. "Wake up," Camacho yelled, "we got work to do!"

But Cummings, who was in bed with Pamela Miller, replied he was too tired for anything, and fell back asleep. David Cooke, however, did go with Camacho, as did Larry Gene Merrell, 38, another friend of Cummings, known familiarly as "The Indian."

A short while later, according to Cummings, he again was awakened, this time by the sound of a crying child—Andre Banks. Gradually, the story of the murder at Sam Wright's house emerged. David Cooke related how Camacho had ordered him to execute the young black man—David Wilburn—who'd walked into the house as they were handcuffing Evellyn. But Cooke, whose criminal history to that point was brief, proved squeamish, so Camacho grabbed the gun and killed Wilburn himself, apparently relishing the task.

Cummings told the FBI agents that he and Pamela Miller left Dallas by car for Lawton on Sunday, May 22. Two days later, they would meet up with Camacho and Cooke in Oklahoma, and part company. Camacho insisted upon taking the dancer with him, lest Miller decide to go to the authorities with what she knew. Cummings said he last saw Miller driving away with Camacho, Cooke and a third man, and that he believed they were headed for Mexico.

On the strength of Cummings' testimony, the FBI obtained a federal kidnapping warrant for George David Cooke, who'd listed an address in Stephenville, west of Fort Worth, when he rented the Dallas apartment with Cummings. Assisted by officer Don Miller of the Stephenville police, Figueroa and Bailey located Cooke and arrested him on August 15 for his role in the Pleasant Grove murder and kidnapping.

Tase Bailey recalls that Cooke at first feigned indifference to his arrest. Cooke's mood changed, however, after he was denied bond, and spent eight days in Lew Sterrett reflecting on the seriousness of his situation. At that point, Cooke decided to accept his attorney's advice to make a deal. He was allowed to plead guilty to one federal count of kidnapping in exchange for what he knew—which was detailed and horrifying.

Cooke was taken before a magistrate at the federal courthouse in Dallas, then spent all night Wednesday, August 24, and into Thursday morning recounting the murder at Sam Wright's to Bailey, Figueroa, and detective Tommy Barnes of the Dallas police.

Two days after killing Wilburn, Cooke said, an agitated Camacho told him "my blue-eyed woman"—Wanda Jackson —had just been interviewed by the FBI—Tase Bailey—and it was time to move. Camacho was furious that the Feds were so close on his tail so soon after the murder. He angrily instructed Cooke to fetch Evellyn Banks and Andre from his apartment (Eddy Blaine Cummings and Pamela Miller already had departed for Oklahoma), and to also locate Spencer Stanley, 26, a sort of brute dogs-body to whom Camacho delegated disagreeable tasks.

Once the group was assembled, Camacho directed Cooke to drive them north to Ardmore, Oklahoma, just across the border from Texas, and about 60 miles southeast of Lawton. Along the way, Camacho kept Evellyn Banks calm with a story of how he knew of a clandestine airstrip near Ardmore, where he'd arranged for her and Andre to be flown to California. When the heat later died down, he assured her, she could return. Banks gave no sign of doubting Camacho.

The next evening, Evellyn and Andre accompanied Camacho, Stanley, and Cooke on a ride out into the Oklahoma countryside. When instead of an airstrip she finally saw the deep grave that Stanley had dug for her and Andre, Banks screamed and fainted.

Tase Bailey shuddered inwardly as Cooke, betraying no emotion, described how son and mother were then murdered. Spencer Stanley, who had been carrying Andre on his shoulders, flung the child into the pit as he and Camacho fired four .380 rounds into Andre's head. Then Evellyn was shoved on top of her boy and executed. A thick layer of cat litter was spread over the two victims.

Then Stanley shoveled dirt back into the hole and pulled some brush over to camouflage the grave.

"We really didn't have a feel for what Camacho was really like until we sat down with David Cooke in the jail," Bailey says. "Once we realized just how evil he was, I guess we made a commitment: 'This guy needs to be caught before more people die. Someone has to stop him.'"

David Cooke had even more to tell.

Two days after giving his statement, as Bailey, Figueroa and DPD homicide detective Barnes were driving him from Dallas to Ardmore to search for the Banks' gravesite, Cooke was asked about Pamela Miller, Eddie Cummings' erstwhile girlfriend.

"We hear Camacho took her to Mexico," said Tommy Barnes, sitting next to Cooke in the back seat.

"No," Cooke corrected him. "She's dead too."

Bailey at the wheel exchanged glances with Jose Figueroa.

"OK, where's her body?"

"You'll never find it."

"Why?"

Bailey could see in his rearview mirror that Cooke was in tears.

"Because we chopped it up and ran it through a tree mulcher."

Two days of bouncing around the back roads of southern Oklahoma were required before David Cooke at last located the remote grave.

It was a typical August afternoon, stultifyingly hot with no hint of a breeze as the lawmen carefully began to dig down in search of the bodies, retrieving spent .380 cartridges as they went.

After two hours of work they were waist deep in the hole. Then agent Brad Farnsworth's shovel hit something that sounded hollow. Farnsworth gently tapped the spot, which gave way in a mini cave-in.

Suddenly, an overpowering reek enveloped the agents, who neutralized the stench by daubing Vick's Vapo-Rub under their noses, and dug on, until they uncovered Evellyn as she had died, lying supine atop Andre. Both were partially mummified by the cat litter.

"I was with the Marines in Vietnam for 13 months," Bailey says. "But nothing ever affected me as that grave did. Andre was just 3 ½. Years before I'd lost a daughter, also 3 ½, in a traffic accident. It really bothered me to see that little kid down in the hole in his pajamas. It was tough."

It got even tougher. Next morning, Sunday, as the group drove southwest back into Texas toward Stephenville, David Cooke hesitantly recounted how Pamela Miller was murdered.

He said that she returned to Dallas from Oklahoma with him and Camacho and Spencer Stanley after the Banks' killings. By now it was early June, and Camacho—mindful that the FBI was searching hard for him—wanted to make a drug score and then head south.

He took a hotel room near Dallas-Fort Worth International Airport, and worked his connections for several days until a drug dealer by the name of Michaels agreed to discuss a possible deal. On Friday night, June 10—Pamela Miller's birthday—Camacho summoned her and David Cooke to a Dallas hotel bar, where he was to meet Mr. Michaels, a heavy-set Anglo in his 40s.

Pamela was in a party mood, Cooke recalled, and drank enthusiastically that night. When Michaels walked into the bar, she blurted, "Hey! I know you. You come into Baby Dolls a lot."

Michaels, who was also a fugitive at that moment, was unamused by Miller's boozy familiarity. He excused himself, and bolted out the back door.

"And that," Bailey says, "apparently really pissed off Camacho."

He dragged a protesting Miller by the arm to the car where he punched her hard in the face—breaking her jaw—and then threw Miller into the back seat.

"Go get Spencer Stanley," he told Cooke.

Though in great pain, Miller taunted Camacho from the back seat, belittling his manhood. He hit her several more times, then reached back with his hand to crush her trachea, apparently believing that would kill her. When Spencer Stanley, seated next to her, reported that Miller was still alive, Camacho ordered the car stopped, pulled the woman out, slammed her to the pavement, then directed Cooke to run over her head, before pitching her once again into the car.

Though unconscious by now, Miller still was not dead. So Camacho repeated the process.

"Let's go to your ranch," he said at last to Cooke, "I'm tired of digging holes."

First they arrived at a townhouse apartment Cooke maintained in Stephenville. Pamela Miller was placed in a 55-gallon drum retrieved from an empty lot next door and deposited on Cooke's back porch. The next day, Camacho ordered that a tree mulcher be rented. Miller's body was trucked in the barrel to Cooke's ranch outside Stephenville, where at Geno Camacho's command Spencer Stanley split Miller with an ax and fed her, piece by piece, into the machine.

It was a macabre experience for Bailey. One day before, he'd excavated Evellyn and Andre in Oklahoma, and then drank a lot of beer that night, trying to get them out of his mind.

Now he had listened to this ghastly story of murder and

mutilation on the drive down from Ardmore with Cooke, only to walk out onto the cow pasture where the mulcher had been put to use.

"We took about three or four steps out into the grass," he says, "and we found a bunch of bone chips with marks on them. There was dried and mummified tissue in the trees, all over the place, covering an area about half the size of a football field. You really can't explain what that is like."

According to David Cooke, Geno Camacho committed one further crime, the rape of a young woman in South Texas, before crossing into Mexico in early July 1988. He traveled south to the town of Arcelia, northeast of Acapulco where, according to intelligence reports, his brother-in-law, Ramiro Pieda owned a trucking company and profited in the marijuana and cocaine trade. Ramiro's sister, Jackie, served as Camacho's common-law Mexican wife.

David Cooke told the FBI he already had visited Camacho in Arcelia by the time he directed Bailey and the other agents to the Ardmore and Stephenville crime scenes. He traveled down to Arcelia, he said, at Camacho's request —they discussed setting up a methamphetamine lab—but Cooke became wary of Camacho's true intents and fled back to the United States.

Cooke's instincts probably served him well. When he later was being held at Lew Sterrett, the Dallas sheriff's intelligence unit intercepted a letter from Camacho in Mexico to a Jamaican drug dealer, also then resident at Sterrett, offering payment if the Jamaican could permanently silence Cooke.

Arcelia and the surrounding area were then under the absolute control of drug traffickers. An unofficial emissary sent down from the Dallas sheriff's office was told by local authorities that nothing short of a military action would succeed in prying Geno Camacho from their midst. As long as he stayed put, Camacho was practically untouchable.

Bailey tried various ploys to lure Camacho back across

the border, but nothing worked. Soon, the previous June and July's sense of frustration returned, amplified now by August's grisly excavations and the grim prospects of ever bringing Camacho to justice.

"I became removed," Bailey recollects. "No communication. One night my wife commented, 'Your demeanor reminds me of what you were like when you first came back from Vietnam.'"

Nor was Bailey the only Bureau employee to be unnerved by what he'd seen and heard. Several members of the Dallas office's support staff, including those who transcribed witness' statements and processed the physical evidence, were afflicted with anxiety attacks, depression, and insomnia. A member of the FBI's Behavioral Science Unit in Quantico, Virginia, an expert in emotional trauma who usually consulted with local police agencies after shootings, was brought to Dallas to counsel them.

Then as hope began to run out, there came a second, even luckier, break in the case.

John Lunt, a Drug Enforcement Administration street agent in Fort Worth, received a telephone call on a Friday in early March 1989, from an informant with intriguing news.

"I'm going to be in Monterrey this weekend," said Lunt's source, "and someone wants to set me up with a guy interested in doing a big weed deal.

All I know right now is that he's a fugitive from the United States."

Lunt urged his source to keep the appointment, and waited eagerly for a report.

On Sunday, the informant called again. "He's using the name Tomas Sanchez, but his real name is Geno. He's wanted on some murders up in Texas.

And he says he will not come to the United States, no matter what."

John Lunt sent his source a picture of Geno Camacho— just to make sure.

Then he contacted Bailey, and the two agents went to work on what they both knew was likely their best chance ever to bring Geno Camacho to justice. They couldn't blow this one.

According to their plan, Lunt's informant bragged to Camacho that he was well connected with mob figures in Kansas City, and that his friends in organized crime were interested in buying 10 tons of marijuana. At the time, marijuana's wholesale price on the border was about $300 a pound: A $6 million deal was in the air.

Bailey, meantime, figured Camacho would call around to check out Lunt's guy. To add a convincing bit of verisimilitude to the plot, Bailey contacted one of his own confidential sources in the Mexican drug trade, alerting the snitch that Camacho might be calling. When he did, Bailey's source assured Camacho he was dealing with the real thing.

"People tell me they know this guy," Bailey's snitch told Camacho about Lunt's snitch. "He's connected and everybody's afraid of him. But he's got a lot of money behind him."

The hook was set, but Camacho still refused to come over the border. He called Lunt's informant several times daily, while the two considered various ways to do the deal. Lunt at one point instructed his snitch to suggest that Camacho consider coming to a supposedly neutral site, the Cayman Islands, where the U.S. agents were prepared to execute what is now called an extraterritorial arrest.

"Back then, we just called it a snatch," Bailey says. Finally, in the third week of March, it was decided that Lunt's snitch would offer Camacho a special lure: $100,000 in earnest money, which he could personally pick up just across the Rio Grande in McAllen, Texas.

On March 27,1989, Lunt's source had urgent news: Greed at last had gotten the better of Camacho's native cunning; he'd agreed to come over. That night, Bailey and Lunt flew to McAllen.

The informant had arranged to meet Camacho on the Texas side of the International Bridge, and then take him to a nearby hotel room to collect his money. To ensure there were no problems with mistaken identities, Lunt's guy sent Camacho a set of clothing to wear that day: turquoise and white Cole-Haan loafers, white shorts, a flowered shirt and a baseball cap which read: Beauty is Only Skin Deep, but Ugly Goes to the Bone. Incredibly, Camacho hadn't balked. Next morning, he loomed onto the International Bridge, clad in the ludicrous ensemble." Here he comes," said an agent on the scene over the phone to Bailey.

"Are you sure?" Bailey answered.

"Yeah, he's wearing those goofy clothes."

To protect their informants, Bailey and Lunt had decided to make Camacho's initial arrest seem to be a routine INS stop of a suspected illegal alien. The FBI and DEA operatives who grabbed the killer as he confidently stepped foot on American soil identified themselves as agents of the Immigration and Nationalization Service, and asked Camacho for identification.

Pleading that he had none, that he was Tomas Sanchez, a tourist from the Valley returning with a bottle of brandy that he showed to the agents, Camacho was told he nevertheless would have to be detained, while his fingerprints were checked. He offered no resistance as he was handcuffed and driven away to the INS lock-up in McAllen.

Bailey at the moment experienced an adrenaline spike." I was just pumped," he recalls. "It was like winning the state football championship. I called Dallas. 'We got the sonuva-bitch!' I told them. I went into the DEA gym and did dips and push-ups just to burn off the energy."

Two hours later, his excitement firmly in hand, Bailey arrived at the INS facility to interview Geno Camacho. He found his quarry serene, imperturbable.

"The fingerprint records say that you are Geno Camacho," Bailey said evenly, savoring this moment above any other in his career.

"Well," Camcho replied, "if that's what the computer says, it must be true." Bailey then showed Camacho his mug shot from Lew Sterrett.

"And is that you?"

"Yes."

"You're under arrest for murder and kidnap."

"I don't know what you're talking about."

Bailey produced a photo of Evellyn Banks in her grave.

"Recognize her?"

"Nope."

Then a picture of Andre.

"How about him? You put four bullets in this little boy's head."

"I don't know anything about him."

"Do you want to tell me about Pamela Miller?"

"Don't know anything about her. I don't want to talk anymore."

End of interview.

Camacho was taken to Lew Sterrett where chief jailer Bob Knowles ordered his prisoner sequestered in a one-man cell, and placed in an orange jumpsuit to make Camacho immediately discernible among his white-clad fellow inmates.

Two officers escorted Camacho wherever he went in the facility. He was convicted and sentenced to death in the spring of 1990 for killing David Wilburn. The moment his sentence was read, Knowles' men put Camacho in handcuffs, leg irons and a belly chain and whisked him away to the Mesquite Airport for an unprecedented direct delivery by helicopter to Death Row in Huntsville.

The following January, 1991, as Camacho awaited federal trial for kidnapping, the still-fugitive Juan Jackson was featured in an *Unsolved Mysteries* segment on television. One viewer, an employee in a Compton, California, bottling plant, recognized Jackson as the co-worker he knew as "Country," for his thick Texas accent, and notified the program. Jackson was arrested the next morning and returned to Texas.

Over the course of the next several months, Juan Jackson was convicted in Federal court for his role in the Wilburn murder, and was sentenced to life without parole in the Federal prison system. David Cooke's plea bargain earned him 24 years in Federal prison, 85% of which must be served before Cooke is eligible for release.

Spencer Stanley received two consecutive life sentences in state court trials in Dallas and Erath County. Eddy Blaine Cummings did eight years of Federal time, and has been released.

Last August, ten years exactly from the day the Federal agents exhumed Evellyn and Andre Banks in Oklahoma, Tase Bailey and his former boss on the violent crimes squad, Joe Hersley, accompanied Pamela Miller's mother, Mickey Miller, to Geno Camacho's execution. The two agents were fulfilling a promise they had made to Miller the day Camacho was condemned in court.

Inside the witness room, she pressed herself against the glass, near to the condemned man as she could get, and chanted with silent satisfaction as Camacho expired, "You're paying. You're finally paying."

The last act of Geno Camacho's life restored Bailey's peace of mind too, although the now-retired agent did reflect at the time on the comparatively gentle manner of the killer's leavetaking." He got a pretty good deal," Bailey thought as he watched Camacho quietly succumb on the gurney. "Any one of his victims, given a choice, would much rather have gone out the way he did than the way they did."

Yet Bailey would not dwell on the point. Hours later, their collective mood of cold contentment still upon them, Bailey, Hersley, and Miller gathered a final time in a

Huntsville motel room to once more salute the moment.

"To a job well done," said Miller, lifting a glass of asti spumante, the sort of gesture she knew Pamela would have appreciated.

"To Pamela," Bailey replied.

All three took a long drink.

Reprinted from the *Dallas Observer*

Murder on Wheels

Walter Scott of Williston, Florida, was a retired Immigration and Naturalization Service official who enjoyed certain genteel pleasures as befit his age and estate.

One such pastime, a weekly favorite, was a leisurely ride with Mrs. Scott and their friends down through the scenic Florida horse farm and citrus grove country to Ocala, where Scott and the rest would enjoy a restaurant supper.

On Saturday night, January 8, 1977, the dinner group was comprised of eight people: Mr. And Mrs. Scott; Eugene Bailey, 77, the well-to-do former mayor of Williston; Bailey's wife and two other couples. They rendezvoused at the Baileys' house that evening, then consolidated themselves into two cars for the 19-mile drive southeast to Ocala. The men rode in Walter Scott's new, four-door Buick. Their wives followed in another vehicle.

It was a chilly, moonless winter night. After dinner at the Holiday House restaurant, Walter Scott walked out to his car in the parking lot to discover that one of his tires was flat and required changing. The women decided to drive on ahead to Williston.

Twenty minutes later, the tire changed, Scott and the others climbed into his Buick and headed home, too. It was about 9:00.

Approximately halfway home on Route 27, a second car drew alongside Scott. Eugene Bailey, sitting in the backseat, would remember hearing a loud bang; he thought they perhaps had been sideswiped, or maybe Scott was having more tire problems. Then Bailey realized that the Buick was slowing and veering to the right off into some scrub growth along the shoulder of Route 27. He also saw that his friend

Walter behind the wheel was slumped forward and covered in blood.

Scott looked very dead, which he was.

As the Buick slewed to a stop, Bailey and the two other men jumped out of the car, fearful and confused. Up ahead, Bailey heard the second car stop. Then, in the dark, a tall angular male, his face disguised in a ski mask, loomed in front of Eugene Bailey, brandishing a pistol. After shouting at the others to get out of the way, the masked stranger opened fire, squeezing four shots at Bailey and hitting him three times, before running back to his car.

Bailey, who miraculously survived the point blank fusillade, lay on the ground and listened as his attacker raced away. He had no idea why he'd been targeted.

Neither did the authorities. The Marion County Sheriff's Office had no workable theory why anyone would attack a carload of old men on their way home from supper. Nor could detectives divine any earthly reason why someone would want Walter Scott or Eugene Bailey dead—although someone certainly seemed intent on killing them. Nothing was stolen, and none of the four men in the Buick was involved in any known personal or business affairs that might explain the bloody ambush.

The available physical evidence at first wasn't much help either. Walter Scott, his autopsy showed, died instantly, from a single shotgun blast to his head.

Among the usual roadside debris found at the scene of the crime, investigators recovered a discarded McDonald's plastic cup bearing fingerprints of unknown origin, and a pair of pantyhose. Neither item would figure in the ultimate solution of the case.

Shell cases found on the ground near the Buick indicated that Eugene Bailey's assailant used a Walther PPK. Also, a small pasteboard address book was discovered along the roadside. None of the names or addresses inside yielded any leads, nor did the detectives attach any significance to the single name written on the back of the book: Clay Taylor.

The case lay in limbo for three years, and might have remained unsolved indefinitely had it not been for one Paul Allen and his penchant for beating up his girlfriend, Maxine Peterson.

Allen, 47 at the time of the murder, was a nickel-and-dime hood, con artist and former bingo hall operator who lived with Maxine, then 51 and a registered nurse, on the outskirts of Gainesville—about 12 miles east of Williston.

After the Scott homicide, Paul and Maxine moved to Opelika, Alabama, where Allen ran his various scams and, from time to time, smacked around Maxine—a habit, together with his drunkenness, that he only recently had developed.

One day, Maxine Peterson tired of the drinking and the abuse and presented herself to authorities with an intriguing string of stories to tell. First, Ms. Peterson said, she had overheard Allen and an Ocala attorney, Raymond Ellis Taylor, Jr., plotting the Scott ambush murder.

"If I can just get rid of that old bastard," Taylor allegedly told Allen, "I'll be set for life."

Next, Peterson continued, Paul Allen left their Gainesville residence before 8:00 on the Saturday night that Walter Scott was killed, and didn't return until 11:00 or afterward. Allen seemed nervous to Maxine that night she said, and he was drinking to excess.

Still according to Peterson, Ray Taylor showed up a couple days later to berate Paul Allen "for getting the wrong guy." Taylor, the irate Maxine recalled, had with him four firearms: two shotguns, a Winchester 30-30 rifle and a Walther PPK.

"We've got to get rid of these guns," she said she heard him tell Allen. "Next time you go fishing, throw these in your favorite fishing spot."

Unbeknownst to Allen, Taylor had already reported the firearms as stolen. Their relationship apparently was not founded on frankness or mutual trust.

Maxine Peterson recounted how Allen wrapped Taylor's four guns in a pink blanket and stowed them under their bed for a couple of days. Then, she recalled, the couple drove west to the Withlacoochee River near Yankeetown on Florida's Gulf Coast, where Allen pitched the weapons into the water.

After hearing Peterson's story, the authorities arrested Paul Allen.

Recognizing that his future was in substantial jeopardy, Allen agreed to trade what he knew—which was extensive and very strange—for 12 years of probation.

According to Allen, the "old bastard" Ray Taylor had been referring to—the man he wanted eliminated—was wealthy Eugene Bailey. Walter Scott had not been the intended target that night.

Taylor, who lived in Williston, rented a small office from Eugene Bailey. He also knew the ex-mayor's son and daughter, and had plotted to insinuate himself into their financial affairs if the old man died.

There was some urgency to the scheme, the snitch Allen explained, because Taylor was going broke.

His third wife, Jane Ann, had just left him, returning with the couple's two children to her hometown of Dayton, Tennessee, about 40 miles north of Chattanooga.

According to authorities, Taylor was tenderly consoled during this difficult period by his Williston legal secretary, Nancy Perez. But the permanent answer to his financial woes, Taylor reasoned, was to gain administrative control of Eugene Bailey's estimated $2.5 million estate.

Observed Gerard King, a former sheriff's detective who led the Scott homicide investigation: "Taylor was a scumbag lawyer with a pretty rotten reputation. He thought that getting rid of Bailey would be the quickest way to make money. It was just a gamble on his part that he'd get hold of the estate."

When prosecutors presented evidence of this motive at trial, Eugene Bailey's son was incredulous. "We never would have given the estate to Ray to handle," he told police and federal agents.

Eugene himself was nonplussed. "I thought he was my friend!" he exclaimed.

Then the story got even stranger.

Paul Allen told the police, and later testified in court, that Ray Taylor, with whom he'd associated in any number of shady deals, including an abortive casino operation, had schemed to murder Eugene Bailey for quite some time.

Nor did the conspiracy end with Allen and Taylor. Suddenly there appeared a third member of the plot—Ray's younger brother William, known as Clay, who was the actual triggerman.

At the time of the murder, Clay Taylor was married and the father of two children, who lived with their mother up in Jacksonville. Tall and lank, a sometime disc jockey, bartender, musician and dance instructor, Taylor had a strong taste for liquor and an even stronger yen for pornography. According to his girlfriend, Patti Randall, he may also have been sexually active with other men.

Miss Randall, a student at the University of Florida in Gainesville—where she first met Clay Taylor—told authorities that Clay once said that if he ever had to run or hide out, he might "go find a fag and live off of him."

Clay Taylor was residing in Chattanooga in December of 1976 when big brother Ray called him down to Florida to help with the hit on Eugene Bailey.

Both brothers were Marine Corps veterans with violent dispositions. In Vietnam, Clay was cited for striking his sergeant. While stationed in California, he came under suspicion for robbery, and was charged by the military for unauthorized possession of a firearm, a .25 automatic.

As Paul Allen told the story, Ray Taylor at first had planned for him and brother Clay to follow Mr. and Mrs.

Bailey home from the Williston Elks Club one night, and to murder them somewhere on the highway. Allen and Clay went out as directed, but couldn't find the Baileys. When they returned to report their lack of success, "Ray was mad as hell at them," reported Gerard King. "Then Clay got mad at him, stormed out, and flew back to Chattanooga."

The conspirators regrouped on January 8. That afternoon, Allen told authorities, Ray Taylor handed out the weapons, and their instructions, at his house in Williston.

Using a car they borrowed from a friend of Patti Randall, Paul Allen and Clay Taylor staked out the Bailey house that evening; this time they wanted to be sure that they knew where the Baileys were headed.

Allen and Taylor shadowed the oldsters down Route 27 to the Holiday House. While the eight friends dined inside, they let the air out of one of Scott's tires.

With Allen at the wheel, they tailed the Buick back up 27 to a pre-appointed stretch of road where Allen pulled even with Scott and Taylor. His identity obscured by a ski mask, Taylor rolled down his window and blasted Walter Scott. They watched as the Buick swung into the trees, and Allen pulled over onto the shoulder just ahead of it.

Taylor meantime tried to jack another shell into the shotgun. It jammed. So he threw the gun to the floorboard and grabbed the Walther PPK. Once Allen had stopped the car, Taylor ran to Eugene Bailey and fired at him four times.

As he ran back to the car, he accidentally dropped Patti Randall's address book, the one with his name written on the back cover.

At trial, the recovered address book not only helped corroborate Paul Allen's testimony, but it also directly tied Clay Taylor to the crime scene.

Later Maxine Peterson led Detective King to the exact spot on the Withlacoochee where she said Paul Allen had thrown the four guns in the water. Divers, including King himself, searched the river bottom for two days with no luck.

King then considered that he might need to consult with an expert on the Withlacoochee's idiosyncrasies of flow and swirl, someone who might have a better guess where the guns had come to rest.

He found Carl Adams, an officer with the Florida Marine Patrol, who not only could guess, but knew where the guns were.

Adams told King that a Seminole Indian artifact hunter named David McCramie had recovered the guns from the Withlacoochee just three weeks after the Scott murder. What was even more helpful to the prosecution was that McCramie had turned in the weapons—including the death-dealing PPK—to the local sheriff. He, in turn, had consulted the National Crime Information Center, only to learn that Ray Taylor had reported the firearms missing.

However, when the authorities tried to return the guns to Taylor—about a month after the Walter Scott murder—they learned he had suddenly relocated to Dayton, Tennessee. There, the attorney had quickly put his marriage back together and gone to work at a fast-food joint while he studied to pass the Tennessee bar.

Because the PPK had been in the water such a short while, it still could adequately be tested to see if it was the weapon used in the assault on Eugene Bailey.

It was.

In May of 1980, Gerard King obtained murder and extradition warrants against all three suspects. Paul Allen was arrested in Opelika. Ray Taylor was taken into custody in Dayton.

In the 40 months since Walter Scott's death, Ray Taylor had passed the Tennessee state bar and metamorphosed from a murderous, womanizing shyster into a popular state prosecutor with a seemingly happy marriage (Jane Ann taught school) and a reputation for being tough on crime.

Needless to say, Ray Taylor's new circle of friends was astonished by the allegations against him. His much less circumspect younger brother Clay—by now estranged from both his wife and Patti Randall—was collared at his Chattanooga workplace, an Arthur Murray dance studio.

Ray Taylor went to trial in Ocala in December of 1980, and was found guilty for his role in the murder and assault. He received as 25-year prison sentence.

After working out his plea bargain, Paul Allen testified against Taylor in court, then moved to West Virginia where he took up a new line of endeavor, fencing hot antiques. A year later, in 1981, Allen died suddenly of a heart attack.

The FBI closely investigated his death, anxious to make sure it was due to natural causes. Triggerman Clay Taylor was then on the loose at that time, and harbored several reasons for wanting his erstwhile partner in crime dead.

Clay Taylor jumped his $20,000 bond soon after his arrest. Authorities still are searching for him.

Reprinted from *Murderers Among Us*

Rampage

Rick Church and Colleen Ritter were sweethearts. Both grew up in solid, respectable middle-class families in Woodstock, Illinois, a village of some 15,000 situated northwest of Chicago, not far from the Wisconsin border.

Rick's father, Gene Church, worked for Commonwealth Edison. So did Colleen's dad, Roy Ritter. Both men also served on the local Little League board. Both families were strongly Catholic.

And the Churches and the Ritters were close friends.

At Marian Central High School, Rick Church was an all-around athlete. A solid five feet, eleven inches and 175 pounds, the handsome young man started at center on the school's state AAA championship football team.

Church's coach, Don Penza, would later describe the youth as "very intelligent, a strong-minded boy, but an excellent, cooperative student."

Colleen Ritter, two years younger than Rick, was a popular and pretty cheerleader. They dated steadily for two and a half years, until the summer of 1988. Then, on one Sunday morning in August, the sort of horrifying, inexplicable violence that always is supposed to happen somewhere else struck the serene town of Woodstock and plunged its residents into anguished astonishment.

After the tragedy, Rick's friends would recall traits that in retrospect seemed ominous to them. "He just had a short fuse," said classmate Mathew Woodruff. "There would be times when he was cool, so good to be around. Then he would turn on you if things didn't go his way. As long as they went his way, he'd be happy."

Friends said that was how Rick's relationship with

Colleen generally rocked along.

Jim Garrelts, another high school friend, remembered a locker-room incident after a basketball game against Round Lake, a rival school.

"We were sharing the dressing room with Round Lake," said Garrets, "And one of their guys started mouthing off. Rick turned around and knocked him cold with one punch. For someone not very big, Rick sure is strong."

Yet no one claimed to see anything in Rick Church's behavior that suggested the possibility of what was to come. He was "a normal kind of guy," said a teammate on the Marian High championship eleven.

He was "a typical high school boy," said Marian High principal, Thomas Landers. "He never did anything or said anything that would give any indication something like this would happen."

But friends did notice a change in Rick Church in 1987, his senior year at Marian, after his parents split up and began divorce proceedings.

The ensuing autumn, as a freshman at Northern Illinois University in DeKalb, the youngster first began to talk of suicide.

According to Mathew Woodruff, also a freshman at NIU that fall, his old high-school friend started getting into bar fights.

Rick's grades, which had been excellent at Marian, quickly deteriorated. Friends recalled he became more possessive and obsessive about Colleen.

He called her incessantly, checked up on her where-abouts, sometimes several times a day. One wall of his dorm room was covered with pictures of her, including one poster-size shot of her posing as rock star Cyndi Lauper.

His grades still plummeting, Rick Church just barely managed to avoid academic dismissal from NIU that year. He returned home in the summer of 1988, moody, telling folks he didn't intend to return to college the next semester.

He found part-time employment as a Little League umpire.

Church lived with his mother Cherry in her apartment, and seemingly avoided his longtime friends and former neighbors through June and into July.

Then calamity hit.

Colleen, who was wearying of Rick's obsessiveness, told him she felt they should start seeing other people. Her parents, who had been worrying about the intensity of the relationship and Rick's obvious jealousy and unusual addiction, had long encouraged their daughter to make the break.

Not long afterward, Church and a group of teenagers went on an outing to Lake Geneva, in Wisconsin.

Sean Noonan, one member of the group, remembered that Rick drank a lot. "And when he got drunk," said Noonan, "he started shouting about how much he hated women and especially Colleen for dumping him. He got loud and obnoxious. One girl told him to quiet down, and he really went off. We had to hold him back from going after her. All the way home in the car he kept mumbling about Colleen and saying, 'How could she do this to me?'"

On Saturday night, August 20, Rick Church went to the Ritter house to plead his case one more time. Between fits of crying and shouting, he vowed he would kill himself if Colleen refused him.

She was diplomatic, but firm. She told friends she thought she had defused the situation by the time Rick left that night.

But a little past five the next morning, one of the Ritters' neighbors was awakened by a shout. "Get out of here!" Screams of terror broke the usually serene neighborhood.

Chris Gehrke, who lived across the street from the Ritters, also heard the screams and looked out his window. He saw a blood-splattered Colleen Ritter racing toward him from her front door. A male figure Gehrke recognized as Rick Church sprinted after her.

Gehrke later told police that Church caught his estranged girlfriend at the pavement and continued his assault.

"He was like a maniac," Gehrke remembered, "hitting her until she stopped moving." Just then, as Gehrke recalled, Church looked up and realized he was being watched.

Gehrke kept staring as the young man ran away around a corner of the Ritter house. He already had disappeared when another neighbor, Jim Meisel, ran into the street to Colleen's broken body.

Meisel, a onetime rescue-squad member, saw a huge bloody gash on the teenager's neck, and began to administer first aid. "I didn't know what had happened," he said later. "It was a bloody mess. Her hair, face and T-shirt were covered with blood. She was conscious, but apparently could not talk. I just got busy on her serious gash wound and did not take much notice of anything else around me." Colleen would survive her wounds; her parents were not so fortunate.

When Woodstock paramedics arrived at the house a few minutes later, they found Mr. and Mrs. Ritter lying close to one another in their living room, savagely beaten and mortally wounded. Both had suffered furious, multiple blows to the head. Roy Ritter had been stabbed repeatedly with a sharp-pronged instrument, possibly a trash stick.

Also in the house was Colleen's little brother, Matthew, and a twelve-year-old friend. Matthew told the police that he and his friend tried to barricade their room with Matthew's bed. Church, said Matthew Ritter to authorities, "came in screaming, thrashing—like an animal" and was about to attack the boys when Colleen ran screaming from the house. It appears that this desperate act saved both her and the boys from her parents' fate.

Following his rampage, Rick Church escaped Woodstock in his mother's 1981 blue Dodge pickup. Despite a massive manhunt, by mid-afternoon that Sunday he'd made it 150 miles northwest across the Wisconsin state line to Wisconsin Dells, where he checked into a motel, paying cash. He left the next morning, appropriating from his room a blanket, some towels, soap and a drinking glass.

A month later, the blue pickup was recovered in a 7-Eleven parking lot in West Hollywood, California. A clerk in the store recognized a photo of Church.

Church eluded capture for more than three years. Part of that time he hooked up with a traveling religious cult, and even did some preaching. But then an off-duty police officer with a good memory and a hunch tipped the FBI and other agencies to arrest Church in November of 1991 in Salt Lake City, Utah.

Salt Lake City police detective Craig Park, 32, spotted Church working at a downtown Salt Lake City restaurant as a cashier and thought the youth looked like a wanted felon on a "Wanted" poster in his office.

When Park returned to his office be dug through a big stack of posters and when he came on the one for Church, he wasn't certain it was the same man. He called the Woodstock officers, who sent him further information and photos.

With that, Park and a supervisor went to Bennett's Pit Barbecue and interviewed Church's boss, who told the officers his employee was going under the name of Danny Lee Carson. He had a forged state ID card that said he had been born in New Mexico in 1958. Park said he knew immediately the ID was a fake. "I knew this guy wasn't 33 years old. It was obvious to me immediately."

Officers then arrested Church at his apartment. He readily admitted his true identity.

The regional manager of the Bennett's Pit chain said Church had been a good employee and was "moving up the ladder."

John Diamond described his employee as "a sharp guy and well-liked. I couldn't believe when I heard the news this morning.

"As far as Richard Church is concerned," he added, "I don't know him. He may have committed the murders they say he did. I know Danny Carson and he couldn't have done the things police say he did."

"America's Most Wanted" and other television shows spotlighted the Church murders a dozen times, but of about 3,000 tips, only 15 reported seeing Church in Utah.

Once extradited back to Illinois, Church cut a plea bargain with McHenry County officials. State's Attorney Thomas Baker vowed to seek the death penalty, but eight months later, in late July of 1992 when Church was tried and convicted, he was allowed to plead for life in prison with no parole.

Church, in admitting guilt in court, said he didn't remember much about the killing spree, only when he picked up a hammer from the Ritters' shed and attacked Colleen. He said he had drunk beer and whiskey all night, smoked marijuana and taken PCP or LSD.

Mr. Baker, the prosecutor, said he accepted the pleas because he was not sure he could get a death penalty conviction. Psychological tests confirmed that Church probably did not remember all of his actions, said Mr. Baker. Colleen and Matthew agreed to the plea bargain, the prosecutor said.

Colleen later married and has a family. She has avoided the public eye.

Reprinted from *Wanted for Murder*

What Her Brother Knew

Dallas County sheriff's detective Larry Forsyth remembers Wednesday, December 23, 1981, began ordinarily enough at the Seagoville substation in the eastern end of the county. The north-central Texas winter sky was pale blue, the temperature mild, and a Christmas party was scheduled for that afternoon. Sgt. Forsyth was appointed the substation's official turkey carver for the occasion. Looking forward to the big meal, Forsyth ate very little for breakfast that morning.

Then the substation radio crackled alive with the ghastly news that a young mother and her child had just been found slain nearby. So much for the Christmas party—and Christmas itself—for Larry Forsyth.

"The first 72 hours after such a murder are so important," he says. "You don't get much sleep trying to get all the leads before they're cold. As a personal note, I also didn't get a chance to eat until ten o'clock that night. We were all awful hungry folks by then."

The bodies were discovered at about 11:45 that morning by Deputy Roy L. Baird. While on routine patrol in a semi-rural area of truck farms scattered among woodlots, creek beds and the occasional hillock, Baird spotted an empty 1978 tan-and-blue Ford Thunderbird parked with its driver's door open on Holloman Rd., a narrow dirt lane three tenths of a mile east of the nearest paved arterial, Lawson Rd.

The car was registered to 30-year-old Roxann Jo Jeeves, an attractive divorcee who had moved to Texas from Oklahoma in April of the previous year. She lived with her son, Kristopher, in a second-story apartment, No. 234, at a complex called The Sussex Place, on Larmanda St. in northeast Dallas. As Deputy Baird approached the abandoned Thunderbird that morning, he noticed a woman's purse and gloves on the front seat. In the backseat there were wrapped Christmas presents, some personal papers, and a blue canvas bag with white trim.

Sensing that something was very wrong, Baird began a general search of the vicinity. In a wooded area 137 feet directly north of Holloman Rd. he found 5-year-old Kristopher lying on his left side. He was clad in blue pants and a blue coat. The boy had been slain with a single .38 caliber bullet to his forehead. His mother lay nearby on her back, covered from her toes to her shoulders with a green blanket. She had been shot once in the cheek, and again in her temple.

From the general appearance of the crime scene, Detective Forsyth surmised that Roxann Jo Jeeves was forced to watch her son's execution before she was killed. At autopsy, Dallas County Chief Medical Examiner Dr. Charles S. Petty found bruises around her neck and stomach, and an inordinate quantity of blood, 100 cubic centimeters, pooled in Jeeves' abdominal cavity. From this evidence, the investigators inferred her killer probably throttled Jeeves into submission, then pinned the woman to the ground with his knee as he shot her.

Ms. Jeeves, like her son, was fully clothed. The keys to the Thunderbird were found in one of her pockets. Neither victim had been sexually assaulted. Neither had been dead for more than an hour, nor had the car been parked on Holloman Rd. for more than 40 minutes. Another deputy reported that he drove by the scene in his cruiser at 11:07 that morning and saw nothing. Crime-scene processing began at 12:25 P.M. No murder weapon was found.

Inside the Thunderbird, however, crime lab technicians recovered good latent fingerprints on the inside of the driver's window. The blue canvas bag in the Thunderbird's back seat potentially was an even more valuable clue. It definitely did not belong to Roxann Jeeves, or to her little boy. Almost certainly it was left by the killer.

Investigators discovered an intriguing array of gear inside the bag, beginning with some screw drivers, knives, and a small bottle labeled lemon extract, but containing formaldehyde. At that time, the best explanation for the formaldehyde was as marinade for marijuana cigarettes to produce what was called a Sherman Stick—ultra-powerful dope that was ultra-dangerous to the health. Says Forsyth: "The majority of people I talked to who'd tried it said they never wanted to do it again. People at our lab say that quite often it leads to brain damage."

Also in the blue bag were a black-knit toboggan cap, with a gold-colored pin attached to it which said, "Super Shit," as well as a small notebook. The name E. Oden was inscribed inside the notebook. After an enormous amount of effort, Larry Forsyth established that E. Oden was Eugene Oden, a local IBM employee who remembered leaving the notebook in his old desk during a company relocation from one part of Dallas County to another.

The last items recovered from the blue bag were several aged (possibly pre-World War II) .38 caliber Remington bullets made of brass, together with a brown leather holster manufactured by Brauer Brothers of St. Louis. A stamped impression on the holster's restraining strap read C O N S T, or perhaps C O 3 1 S T. The lettering was very faint.

According to a Brauer Brothers employee contact by the Dallas County investigators, the company once supplied this type of holster to the military by the thousands, but discontinued the model in 1952. It seemed quite likely that the bullets and holster were stolen, together, along with the missing murder weapon, undoubtedly a pistol. Larry Forsyth believes that to find their owner—and also to solve the mystery of how Eugene Oden's notebook wound up in the blue bag—probably would bring him much closer to identifying the killer.

"I've always felt that the holster and pistol had been passed down from somebody's grandfather," he says. "And I think they came out of a burglary. I always hope that somebody will call and say, 'That's my holster!' Then I could go back and start working on that. That holster haunts me—that and the notebook. How the hell did that notebook get from that office building, to where that mama and baby were killed, and in that bag?"

Neither sex nor robbery seemed to be motives in the case, and nothing that the sheriff's office learned in the crucial early hours of its investigation brought detectives any closer to understanding who someone would want to murder Roxann Jo Jeeves and little Kristopher. They discovered that she was a native of Jamestown, New York, in the far western portion of the state, not far from the Pennsylvania border. Roxann Jo Jeeves had married (retaining her maiden name) and moved to Oklahoma City, where she worked for an insurance company for a couple of years. Her ex-husband, Kristopher's father, still resided there. He was not a suspect.

In Dallas, the detectives learned that Jeeves led a moderately active social life. She played on a women's baseball team in the summer and enjoyed dancing in country-and-western joints with names like "No Whar But Texas" and "The Cockeyed Cowboy." Her boyfriend of the past 12 months, Jimmy Hoskins, told police he had last spoken to her, by telephone, at about 10 on the night before her murder. Jimmy Hoskins was at work the next morning when Roxann and Kristopher were murdered.

His mother, 53-year-old Louise Hoskins, told investigators that she spoke with Roxann, also by telephone, at 10:00 AM on the twenty-third, less than two hours before mother and son were found dead. According to Mrs. Hoskins, Roxann and Kristopher were due at her workplace, Kraft Foods in nearby Garland, at 11:00. It was Kristopher's birthday. As a special treat, Mrs. Hoskins was going to take the boy on a tour of the plant. Still another acquaintance, 37-

year-old Danny Binion, recounted to Forsyth that he had visited the Jeeves apartment on the night of the twenty-second. Before leaving at about 10, said Binion, he noticed that Roxann had placed a red box full of car tools near her front door. When Binion asked about the toolbox, she explained that she intended to put it in her Thunderbird's trunk the next morning, "in case I have car trouble." Danny Binion confirmed Louise Hoskins's account. He recalled Roxann telling him that she and Kristopher planned to meet Mrs. Hoskins at Kraft Foods around 11:00 the next morning. Then, according to Binion, Roxann was going to bring Kristopher to Binion's club, the King's X, before taking the boy for the last of his birthday treats, a movie matinee.

One of the first witnesses to provide Detective Forsyth with something substantive, was 19-year-old Patricia McAvey, Roxann Jeeves' neighbor at The Sussex Place. At about 10:30 on the morning of the twenty-third, McAvey walked out of her apartment to see Kristopher struggling down the stairs toward his mother's car with a big red toolbox. McAvey, on her way to a doctor's appointment with her own infant son, asked Kristopher if he needed any help. The boy declined, explaining that he thought he was big enough to wrestle the cumbersome toolbox downstairs all by himself. She said she then hurried off across the parking lot toward her car. Partway there, McAvey turned around to see something she found disquieting, a black male accompanied by a dark-complected Indian female, who seemed to be approaching Kristopher Jeeves in a furtive manner. "They were looking around to see if anyone was watching," McAvey said.

The unwholesome-looking duo unnerved Patricia McAvey. "She didn't feel like these people belonged in her apartment complex," says Forsyth, although McAvey added that Kristopher Jeeves seemed to recognize the man. "When she got to her car, she looked back one more time and this time she saw the black man carrying the toolbox in one hand

and holding Kristopher's hand with the other. All three of them—the Indian woman, also—were headed in the opposite direction around the building to the parking lot. That's the last she saw of them."

Patricia McAvey sat down with a police artist to produce a sketch of the suspect male. Over the coming days, the drawing was widely reproduced in the Dallas news media. According to McAvey, the man was about five feet, nine inches tall, and weighed 180 pounds, possibly more. He looked to be in his early-to-mid thirties. His black hair was cut short. She remembered he wore sunglasses, a dirty white T-shirt under a blue jogging top, and light brown pants covered with grease smears.

The suspect's companion presented an equally derelict aspect. McAvey described her as a squat five-five, about twenty-five years old. The woman's hair, the witness said, was short and brown and frizzy. She wore ill-fitting tan slacks. It appeared that recently someone had smacked her around, giving the woman a black eye.

The next significant witness was Don Crawford, who worked in a gas station not far from The Sussex Place. Within hours of the murders, Crawford notified the sheriff's investigators that he had pumped gas that morning for Roxann Jeeves; according to her credit card receipt, $31.00 worth. Crawford remembered that Ms. Jeeves was at the wheel of the Thunderbird and that she said nothing more than "Fill it up," at the station.

Sitting quietly next to her in the front passenger seat was a black male who looked to be somewhere between 30 and 35 years of age. The attendant went on to explain to deputy W.L. Mayes that he saw a little boy, maybe three or four years old, standing up in the back seat. The tyke was wearing a blue coat, and blue pants. No one else was in the vehicle.

Assuming the black male whom Don Crawford saw in

Roxann Jeeves' Thunderbird is the same individual Patricia McAvey saw with Kristopher that morning, his female companion, whomever she was, seems to have vanished. Besides Larry Forsyth, another principal investigator on the case was deputy R.W. Veatch, who turned up a number of witnesses. One, twenty-year-old Tamera Burton, reported that just about the same time deputy Baird discovered the abandoned Jeeves Thunderbird on Holloman Rd., she saw a man she only could describe as "dark" sprinting out of the brush nearby. "He was running as fast as he could," Burton said in her statement. The subject wore "dark clothing with a greenish look to it."

Another of Veatch's witnesses, thirty-four-year-old Michael Dean Daniel, worked at a water-treatment plant about a half-mile from the murder scene. Daniel told Veatch that when he left work at noon on the twenty-third, as he drove across Holloman Rd., a black man ran out from behind a vacant house and tried to flag him down, as if he needed a ride.

Daniel said he drove on, but was later able to describe the subject. He was, recalled Daniel, in his twenties, about five-eleven, and of medium build. The man also had facial hair. Despite his frantic attempts to get Veatch's attention, he kept his left hand hidden inside the pocket of an olive-drab military jacket.

Daniel's descriptions were consistent with those of Jim and Marcella Hicks, Seagoville residents who reported to Veatch that they also were driving in the vicinity of the murder scene at about noon that day. Jack Hicks remembered seeing a black man trying to hitch a ride. The individual was about five feet, ten inches tall, said Hicks, of medium build and somewhere in his twenties. Hicks recalled that the man wore dark clothes and had a stubbly beard. Marcella Hicks concurred, adding that the hitchhiker's hair was cut in a short Afro, and that he wore a "drab-green" military-style jacket. Both Hickses and their passenger that day, Marsha Youker, said they noticed that the man kept his left hand in his jacket pocket. All three believed they'd recognize the subject were they to encounter him again.

As Detective Forsyth, Deputy Veatch and the rest of the Dallas County sheriff's investigators through the 1981 Christmas weekend, the flow of substantive leads inexorably slowed, even though the local press continued to show the police composite sketch of the suspect. Schepp's, a civic-minded local dairy, also offered a $10,000 reward for information leading to the arrest of Roxann Jo and Kristopher Jeeves' killer. One of the last of the useful early witnesses was 35-year-old Katie M. Christian, a gas station attendant like Don Crawford who contacted the sheriff's office on Monday, December 28, five days after the murders. Christian worked at a Mobil station about six miles due west of the crime scene. According to her, at about noon on the twenty-third a black man about five feet, eight inches tall, medium build, wearing a green army jacket and green cap, walked into the station and asked to use the inside telephone. After placing his call, the subject loitered around the station for an hour or so, coming inside at one point for a drink of water. The last Ms. Christian saw of him, he was headed north, on foot.

All sensational crimes provoke deluges of anonymous tips to the authorities, and the Jeeves murders were no different. Although most such calls come from pranksters, cranks and the like, there often are concrete leads to be followed, or facts to be gleaned that may cast the crime in a new light. In the Jeeves case, many of the callers suggested that if the detectives dug hard enough, they'd find a drug connection in the killings. The discovery of the formalde-hyde in the killer's blue canvas bag also pointed to some sort of drug connection, as did the highly suggestive testimony of Kevin Long, another of Roxann Jo Jeeves' neighbors at the Sussex Place.

Several weeks after the homicides, Long was involved in

a fracas at the complex. It was a matter of routine for sheriff's investigators to ask Long if he knew anything about the Jeeves' slayings. "I wish I could help you guys," Long replied. "But I can't." The detectives started leaning on him. After three days of their intense attention, Long finally exclaimed, "Look! I'm in a real jam here. But if you give me your words that you won't cause me any problems, I'll tell you what I know."

Kevin Long, it turned out, was a parolee. What he had to report could put him back in jail. According to Forsyth, Long said he remembered seeing a black man in the complex who fit the suspect's description. In fact, the man had come to Long's door about three or four days before the murder, asking to borrow his battery jumper cables. Long didn't own any, but as they chatted at his apartment door, the stranger picked up the pungent aroma of marijuana being smoked within. "Hey man, who's got the reefer?" he asked. Long answered that he did, and some of it might be for sale. As they spoke, the stranger introduced himself as "G-Man." He said he might be in the market for some dope. When Kevin Long shook his hand, he noticed G-Man was wearing a horseshoe-shaped ring, and that there was a long pink scar on his right hand. The rest of what Long had to say was even more provocative. He told Forsyth that the selfsame G-Man returned to his door on the morning of the murders and purchased a baggie of marijuana. Finally, says Forsyth, "Long told us something about the clothing we've never made public. Something the other witnesses noticed. Something unusual."

Kevin Long's information, consistent with a drug-related theory of the murders, still shed no light on another nagging point. Neighbor Patricia McAvey felt that little Kristopher recognized the suspect that morning. If she was right, then what, or who, could have been the connection?

One distinct possibility was Roxann Jo Jeeves' brother, Kurt, who had come to Dallas from Jamestown the previous summer, and lived with his sister and nephew for a few weeks. Some of the telephone tipsters mentioned Kurt by name. Others went so far as to say he had two distinguishing habits: One was to smoke dope regularly, and the other was a preference to associate with blacks. For some reason, whites were nearly excluded from Kurt Jeeves' circle of acquaintances.

On January 21, 1982, 29 days after the murders, Detective Forsyth traveled about 125 miles southwest of Dallas to Ft. Hood, the U.S. Army base near Killeen, Texas. There, he interviewed PFC Kurt Jeeves. Roxann Jo's brother conceded he had been in the dope trade. He told Forsyth that Brantley Wood, a black man who lived quite close to Roxann at The Sussex Place had "fronted" him four kilos of marijuana to sell. When Kurt didn't move the product quickly enough, he said, Wood came to the Jeeves apartment and angrily demanded the marijuana's return. Kurt Jeeves also remembered Wood answering his own door with a knife in his hand. His explanation was that someone had just burgled his place and made off with part of his dope stash.

Forsyth asked Jeeves the obvious question: Was there some reason that he preferred the company of African-Americans to whites? "I got a strange reaction," says Forsyth. "When I asked him if any of his black friends had anything to do with this, he jumped up and said, 'You're not gonna put a guilt trip on me! I didn't have anything to do with my sister's murder, and I'm through talking to you.'" As it turned out, this conversation was the first and last Detective Forsyth would have with Kurt Jeeves.

By the time he got back to Dallas that day, there was a call awaiting him from Jamestown. It was Kurt Jeeves' father, demanding that the Dallas County Sheriff's Office leave his son alone. Kurt Jeeves subsequently shipped out to Germany, where he was tried and convicted for a drug offense. The Army returned him to the United States in 1984. He served time in the Louisville, Kentucky, stockade before being dishonorably discharged.

"He was kicked out of the Army and given his back pay," says Forsyth. "Almost immediately, he into a black part of Louisville to score some marijuana, and was killed because he flashed a big roll of bills. A group of blacks was arrested and convicted, but we could find no connection whatsoever to our case." Since then, the only significant development in the case came in 1988 with a Crime Stoppers television broadcast. After the show, a viewer called in to say that on December 23 he'd seen a black man stop to pick up another black man near the Mobil station where Katie Christian worked.

So why were Roxann Jo and Kristopher Jeeves killed? One possibility is that Mr. G-Man bought his dope, soaked it in formaldehyde, smoked a Sherman Stick and went off on a psychotic tear. More likely, the killer had some sort of beef, probably with Kurt, and killed his sister and nephew as a payback, or warning. Yet that explanation suggests a thinking criminal, and this killer did not fully consider his crime. It was rash to be seen with his victims in the daytime, and then to murder them with no apparent plan to escape, unless he'd intended to take the Thunderbird, and had been scared off by Deputy Baird.

And what about his left hand? Had he injured it, and how? None of these questions likely ever will be answered unless Detective Forsyth someday gets his man.

Today, as the top lieutenant at the Dallas County sheriff's office, Forsyth commands many criminal investigations, but this one—the files stacked underneath his desk to this day—remains the one he'd like most to solve.

"You never know," he said recently. "Something might eventually turn up, give us a break. You just can't give up."

Reprinted from *Murderers Among Us*

Double-wide Homicide

Thirty-two year old Shirley McAvoy was a mess; depressive (possibly bipolar), alcoholic, recently separated from her husband, Brian, and barred from contact with her two daughters, aged 8 and 12, after several episodes of physically abusing them.

Shirley spent most of her days alone with her two dogs, a mixed shepherd-husky puppy and a longhaired black cocka-poo, in her three-bedroom double-wide house trailer on a 2-acre tract in Pittsfield, Maine, about 25 miles due west of Bangor.

When night came, Mrs. McAvoy usually went bar-hopping in Pittsfield and the neighboring working-class towns in south central Maine. "Since her separation she hung out in bars a lot," said Maine State Police detective Dale Lancaster. "She fancied herself something of a party girl."

Often as not, Shirley dragged home a new friend for breakfast, or spent the night at his place. Sex, of course, was usually the upshot of these boozy encounters, but it was not necessarily their object—at least not McAvoy's.

According to friends, she was consumed by the subject of intercourse even while she detested the act itself. Detective Lancaster speculates that this particular wrinkle in her psyche may have cost Shirley her life.

On Thursday, August 8, 1990, she invited several friends to a party at her trailer. On hand for the event was a stranger, maybe in his middle thirties, who had riveting pale blue eyes, and spoke with a southern accent.

His name was Jerry, as he told some people, or was it Don? That's what others recalled.

"He manufactured different stories about himself," said

Lancaster. "He seemed to be what anyone wanted him to be."

Jerry, or Don, was an Air Force mechanic from Virginia, or a mill hand working down the road in Millinocket. All that the witnesses could agree on was that he talked of wanting to become a Navy SEAL. He must have seen the movie. Shirley wasn't much more forthcoming about him. She didn't say where she picked him up, only that he'd been staying with her for three days, and that theirs was not a sexual relationship. Jerry was sleeping in a separate bedroom, she said.

The last person to see Shirley McAvoy alive was a process server, who came to her door with some divorce papers from Brian at 5:00 P.M. the next day, August 9. The following morning, Saturday, Shirley's neighbors saw Jerry driving away from the double-wide, apparently alone, in Shirley's 1990 red Oldsmobile Cutlass Supreme. Late that afternoon, Jerry rammed the Cutlass into a Mercedes 360 on Boston's crowded Southeast Expressway. The accident was little more than a fender-bender. The Mercedes driver later told detectives from Maine that Jerry calmly produced insurance cards from the Olds' glovebox, and coolly handed them over. He seemed unruffled by the incident.

Massachusetts is a no-fault auto insurance state. Assuming that the man in front of him was Brian McAvoy, the other driver, an attorney, didn't ask for identification. He assumed he could get a repair estimate and then forward it to McAvoy in Maine.

Ten days later, McAvoy in fact did receive the estimate by mail from Boston. It was going to cost $1600 to fix the Mercedes. Baffled by this letter, McAvoy called Shirley at her trailer, but received no answer. His next call was to the Pittsfield police.

For the next several weeks, the case was treated as a routine missing person matter; the local authorities did not go to any particular length to locate Mrs. McAvoy, whose lifestyle was well-known to the community. One reasonable presumption was that Shirley and Jerry had taken off on a trip together, which in fact would prove to be the case.

In early October, with Shirley (and her dogs) still missing, Brian McAvoy decided to visit her trailer to shut off the water and bleed the pipes lest an early freeze burst them

Inside, he sensed something was amiss. When she and Brian split the previous January, she had impulsively jettisoned all their furniture in favor of new chairs and tables that would not remind her of her former life.

Shirley even went so far as to buy new kitchen knives. But Brian had been around enough to be familiar with his ex-wife's new home furnishings, and these didn't look right. For one thing, the place seemed altogether too tidy; Shirley didn't keep house that way. He saw that the kitchen curtains now hung in the living room, and that Shirley's wall coatrack had been moved, as had her living-room couch.

Curious about all this, McAvoy walked over and removed one of the coats; there were small dark-red splotches on the wall behind it. Then he slid the couch to its original place, and discovered it had been concealing a red crusted stain, roughly three feet long by two feet wide. Brian McAvoy called the police once more. With the discovery of the blood stains-type O, Shirley's type—and the consequent presumption of foul play, the Maine State Police entered the case.

An NCIC check on the missing Oldsmobile revealed it had been stopped for some sort of traffic violation in Florida on August 14, four days after Jerry was last seen driving away in the car from Pittsfield. Further investigation placed the car itself in Georgia. It had been stolen from a parking lot in Florida, repainted, and sold.

A police sketch of Jerry was commissioned and released to the media. A fuller explanation of Shirley McAvoy and her dogs' fate awaits Jerry's capture, which won't be easy given the paucity of information about him.

Maine authorities do not even have his fingerprints.

Detective Lancaster thought it a good guess, however, that Shirley drank with Jerry, who became sexually aroused. "She might have heated this guy up," said the detective, "and then said, 'No,' and that made him snap."

Reprinted from *Murderers Among Us*

Fatal Encounter

"Mrs. Wood," read the Manatee County Sheriff's Office Incident Report, "stated that on October 8, 1983, her husband got mad at her son and began beating him about the head and face. She further stated that he had the boy in a head lock and when she was going to call the police he threatened to snap the boy's neck."

Cynthia Ruth Wood, 33, of Bradenton, Florida, at last had had enough. For four years she had endured alleged abuse, intimidation, even extortion by her husband, Barry T.D. Wood. As she accused him in a court filing: "The Husband... repeatedly perpetrated acts of physical abuse upon the wife... such acts as holding a pillow over the Wife's face in such a manner as to cause the Wife to be unable to breathe to the point of becoming semi-conscious, and has struck the Wife on numerous occasions about the face and body with his fists and with numerous weapons, including a 2-by-4 piece of wood. The Husband has struck the minor child of the Wife... about the face and head on numerous occasions with his fists, a hammer and, on one occasion, a 2-by-4, for such things as not eating all the meal prepared for him and for failing to do chores about the house. The Husband has a practice of punching said child in the stomach to avoid obvious bruises and other marks. Said child's teachers are aware of the fact that he has appeared in school with bruises and abrasions due to the physical abuse by the Husband."

Somehow, Cindy Wood had found the courage to risk Barry's wrath by fleeing the horror she described. The day after he allegedly threatened to snap 14-year-old Tommy's neck, Cindy drove her oldest boy and the Woods' two children, 4-year-old Barry, Jr., and Jeanette Trinity, 2, to the Tampa airport, intending to escape with the children back to her native Pennsylvania. As she waited for her flight to freedom, an anonymous male telephoned the airline, claiming that someone was kidnapping his children on the flight to Philadelphia. A short while later, a second anonymous male telephoned a bomb threat to the airline. Cindy was not surprised when Barry then showed up in person at the airport. He was detained and questioned while the plane was searched. No bomb was discovered, so Mrs. Wood at last got aboard the jet with her three kids and flew off to freedom and the hope of a new life.

About a month later, Barry Wood filed for divorce, and headed north by car from Florida to Philadelphia. As Cindy would later allege in a petition, Barry and his daughter by a previous marriage, Denise, accosted her and the two smallest children on the street. She was pushed to the ground, according to her criminal complaint, and the kids were snatched away from her. Barry returned to Bradenton. Cynthia followed, determined to get little Barry, Jr., and Jeanette Trinity back. Nearly penniless, she found a lawyer to file her custody petition for free, and then dug in for the legal battle.

In her various court filings, Cindy repeated her allegations of violence by Wood against her and the kids. She also claimed that in 1982 her estranged husband had physically forced her to sign away her share of their real property in Bradenton—land and a house for which Barry subsequently realized a $40,000 return when he sold them. Wood fought on. When her husband denied all her charges, and alleged in his reply that she was hallucinating, Cindy found a psychiatrist who examined her and declared her mentally competent.

Gradually, she began to make some headway in the case, beginning with visitation rights. According to her friends, by early June 1984 Cindy Wood's outlook had brightened considerably. Her husband was about to go on trial for his alleged physical abuse of Tommy. On Friday, June 1, she told her niece, Shirley Wood, that a custody report was due shortly from the Florida Department of Health and Rehabilitative Services, and that she understood the state strongly would recommend that she, not Barry, be given custody of the two little ones.

Then came a fatal encounter.

Michael Santini was a native of Massachusetts who grew up in Texas. Trisha Earley, a onetime friend, would tell Bradenton Herald reporter Joanne Fiske that Santini was a lifelong loser. "He seemed to screw up a lot," said Earley. "He couldn't keep a job. He reminded me of a little boy, somewhat naive, lost."

Santini matured into a violent adult. In 1978, while stationed by the U. S. Army in Frankfurt, Germany, the 20-year-old private was convicted of rape and sentenced to two years in the stockade. "He said he was never going to spend time in jail again," Ms. Earley told Fiske. "If it came down to killing himself or going back to jail, he said he'd kill himself."

On the afternoon of May 2, 1983, while living in the Houston suburb of Sugarland, Santini walked into a local convenience store, grabbed a female clerk by the wrist. shoved a knife in her face and demanded the store's cash. He then fled in his tan Chevy station wagon. The clerk, who was not physically injured, took down Santini's license tag number, which resulted in his arrest just five hours later.

When the police assured Santini that everything would be all right if he just told the truth, he did. According to Trisha Earley, it was a shock and major disappointment to the young man when he was charged with aggravated burglary. That October, about the time Cindy Wood was fleeing Florida with her children for Pennsylvania, Michael

Santini was fleeing Texas for Florida.

By the time a judge issued a fugitive warrant for him, Santini was working as a janitor at the Gulf Tides Hotel in Longboat Key, directly across from Bradenton via a causeway. He called himself Charles Michael Stevens. Santini kept the janitor's job for a month before he was fired, on November 14, after various cleaning supplies and articles of furniture disappeared at the Gulf Tides. Next month, he was hired as an electrician's helper at Bradenton Electric Co., where Santini worked until April.

Meantime he moved in with Pam Kincaid, a coworker at the Gulf Tides, who was a single mother and an acquaintance of Cindy Wood. Kincaid's residence on 36th Avenue Drive West was just a short distance from Cindy Wood's new workplace, the Cape Vista Child Care Center. Pam Kincaid's children played at Cape Vista while their mom was at work.

Samuel L. Harding of Bradenton, our next new character, met Santini, or Charles Stevens as Harding knew him, about this time, and sold Stevens a motorcycle, on time. Harding's mistake was to allow Santini/Stevens use of the bike before he'd fully paid for it.

On April 10, with Pam Kincaid's brother Bob aboard the machine with him, Santini/Stevens led Florida Highway Patrol Trooper Tim Johnson on a 20-mile chase through Sarasota and Manatee counties at speeds of up to 90 mph. He ran several stoplights and at one point barely missed colliding with a woman pushing a baby carriage. "He drove like his life depended on it," Trooper Johnson later told Joanne Fiske, "and now I know why. He had good reason to run."

Johnson couldn't catch Santini, but he did get the bike's license number. That night, Manatee county deputies arrested Samuel Harding for reckless driving, despite his protests that the man he knew as Charles Stevens was their culprit. Harding spent the night in jail before Trooper Johnson saw him in the lockup and realized that they'd put wrong man behind bars. The following year, Harding sued several of the officers involved in his case for false arrest. Santini never was arrested in connection with the bike incident, even though Samuel Harding told the Florida Highway Patrol that he lived with Pam Kincaid. "We don't have the manpower to follow up and stake places out for somebody in violation of a minor misdemeanor," John explained to the Herald.

"If we had known it was Santini, we sure would have done everything to get him." On April 25, Santini-as-Stevens went to work as a receiving clerk at the Longboat Key Club, a resort.

About this time, Cindy Wood told her niece Shirley about a tall, blond male she'd met at the Cape Vista Child Care Center. Several times when he came by to pick up Pam Kincaid's kids, he asked Cindy out on a date. She refused.

Charles Stevens and Pam Kincaid split the sheet in early June of 1984. On Monday, June 4, he paid Ms. Kathryn Shipman two weeks' advance rent for a room at 690 Jungle Queen Way on Longboat Key. Santini appears to have come into some money.

"He was a very quiet person," Kathryn Shipman would remember. "He had some nice luggage and a nice leather, or suede, jacket. They looked like they were expensive." That evening, Cindy Wood called Shirley Wood to report that the man who'd been asking her for dates at the day-care center now said he had information for her about Barry Wood, a story that might be useful to her in the custody fight. Cindy Wood must have thought it peculiar that this stranger would know something about Barry. But she swallowed whatever suspicions she had and reluctantly agreed to have dinner with the man. Tommy Wood said that the man who came to pick up his mother at 9:30 that night answered Charles Stevens' description.

Cindy Wood was never seen alive again.

Santini-Stevens hastily left town the next day, leaving

much of his personal property, including his bottle of peroxide, in the room he'd just rented from Kathryn Shipman. A later search of his desk at the Longboat Key Club revealed scribbled directions, in Santini's hand, to Cindy Wood's house, plus a description of her car and her license tag number. Sometime during that day, say police, Santini also confessed to Pam Kincaid that he had killed Cindy Wood the night before. No details of the confessions were released.

Just before Santini-Stevens disappeared for good that day, Shirley Wood called a missing-person report into the Manatee Sheriff's Office. Shirley told the sheriff's deputy that she suspected Cindy had met with foul play, and shared her belief that her uncle Barry somehow was mixed up in it. At 5:05 that evening, Barry Wood contacted the sheriff's office himself.

Wood had heard how Tommy described the man who came for his mother, and insisted to the deputy that Cindy would not "hang around with any man answering the description given by Tommy." Wood asked repeatedly where Tommy was.

The deputy with whom he spoke (identified only as D. Turner on the police log) then went home, only to hear a half hour later that Wood had called him four times at the sheriff's office, and left a number for Turner to return the calls.

"I contacted him," Turner recorded. "He told me that his wife was 'heavy into alcohol and hung out with a whole bunch of men.' He again asked where Tommy was... He also told me that he had hired a detective, and indicated that he knew me, and wanted to work exclusively with me."

Deputy Turner's notes further indicate that Barry Wood suggested the only man Cindy knew who answered Tommy's description was "Charles Michael Stephens." [sic]. Next day, Cindy's brother Joseph Wesley of Newton, Pennsylvania, telephoned the sheriff's office to report that he, too, had been contacted by Barry Wood "requesting information on the location of his son, Tommy Wood," the sheriff's report read. "Mr. Wesley believes Barry Wood could be responsible for the disappearance of Cindy..."

Barry Wood was back on the phone to deputy Turner on June 8. "During the interview," according to Turner's notes, "he again started to describe his wife's character and stated that 'she was heavy into drugs and hung out in various bars'... Wood continued his assault on Cindy's character through the next day when, at about 3:30 in the afternoon, her body was found floating face down in a drainage ditch. She was identified from fingerprint records.

Her autopsy showed that she'd been strangled—authorities would not reveal exactly how—but her body bore no other marks of physical injury. Nor had Cindy Wood been sexually assaulted. Nine days later, a first-degree murder warrant was issued for "Donald Michael Santini, aka Charles Michael Stevens et al."

Authorities in Manatee County say they believe the Wood murder was a paid hit, but refuse to elaborate as to why. Although there have been various sightings over the years, Santini remains a fugitive.

Barry Woods left Bradenton with little Barry and Jeanette. According to Joe Wesley, Cindy's brother, Tommy moved to Pennsylvania to live with an aunt. His mother's fitting eulogy, and vindication, was written the week after her murder. On June 14, Martha Hauber, a counselor with the Florida Dept. of Health and Rehabilitative Services, wrote a letter to the Wood vs. Wood divorce case judge, Nick J. Falsone.

"Due to the alleged murder of Cynthia R. Wood," wrote Hauber, "we feel it is appropriate to close the above case without writing a report." She continued. "We found Cynthia R. Wood to be a very warm, capable devoted mother whose children seemed well adjusted in her home and to have an excellent relationship with her. The relationship between her fourteen-year-old son and the three and five year old children of her second marriage also appeared to be exceptional as they as seemed to enjoy being together so much but they respected each other as individuals rather than being dependent on them."

The coda to Cindy Wood's sad travail was written by Joanne Fiske in the Bradenton Herald. Barry Wood wanted his wife's body cremated. Her brothers wanted her to be buried, according to her wishes, near her mother's grave in Pennsylvania. The brothers' attorney, Herbert Berkowitz, obtained an injunction to prevent the coroner from releasing her body to Wood until the matter could be resolved.

"It was just tremendously important to them," Berkowitz said. "They knew she had a terrible relationship with him and it was meaningful to them that they didn't leave her in his grasp."

A judge found that Wood had a greater right to her remains. The family reluctantly agreed to allow Mrs. Wood to be buried in Manatee County as long as she was not cremated. On Aug. 3, nearly two months after her body was discovered, Cindy was buried.

Reprinted from *Murderers Among Us*

The Toy Texan

According to his family and close friends, rare book dealer and historian John ("Johnny") Holmes Jenkins III, 49, of Austin, Texas, was in good spirits on the bright April Sunday in 1989 when Jenkins climbed into his gold Mercedes and drove southeast 30 or so miles from Austin into Bastrop County. Jenkins certainly gave no indication of despondency or depression, emotions that in any case seemed utterly alien to him. Jenkins, the author of a well-respected bibliography of Texas historical tracts and treatises, entitled *Basic Texas Books*, was at work on the biography of Edward Burleson, a patriot of the Texas revolution. He believed he had at last pinpointed where Burleson's father was buried. Jenkins was headed down into Bastrop County to see if he was right. Johnny Jenkins' frame of mind that day is important. Con Keirsey, then sheriff of Bastrop County, believed that the bookseller himself was responsible for the large bullet hole discovered later that same Sunday in the back of Jenkins' head when his body was recovered near a boat ramp on a turbid stretch of the Colorado River in Bastrop County.

If Sheriff Keirsey's right, then Johnny Jenkins certainly selected an unconventional and melodramatic way to kill himself, which would have been in character. However, the Bastrop County authority who then determined official causes of death, Justice of the Peace B.T. Henderson, thought someone besides Johnny Jenkins pulled the trigger. Many who knew the dead man concur. "If that sheriff had been in a room for one minute with Johnny Jenkins," one of Jenkins' employees told a reporter, "he'd know he's barking up the wrong tree. He'd know about the force of his personality, his confidence, his assurance to himself, and to those around him that any problem could be overcome. What it gets down to is that the sheriff didn't know Johnny Jenkins." But maybe no one did. "The truth is," said one acquaintance in the book trade, "that he was a very complex person, not a simple man."

Johnny Jenkins had eclectic business interests. He sank considerable sums into a non-remunerative oil-drilling enterprise. He once backed a feature-length horror movie, Mongrel, which was humanely destroyed soon after its release. Jenkins also had another name, Austin Squatty, his sobriquet when he competed in the company of world-class poker players in Las Vegas and elsewhere. Jenkins wasn't called Austin Squatty because he waddled when he walked, although he did. And according to an article by Calvin Trillin in The New Yorker magazine, they didn't call him Austin Squatty because he was short, perhaps no taller than five feet, six inches. No, Trillin's sources suggested the name derived from Jenkins's poker-table habit of sitting cross-legged, "the way Indians in movies sit around the campfire," as Trillin put it. In other venues, Jenkins was referred to as the Toy Texan.

It is unclear whether Johnny Jenkins ever won much money playing cards; there has been peculation that he was, in fact, a poor player and deeply in debt to unsavory elements in Nevada and maybe New Jersey. If so, then Johnny Jenkins's real cause of death could have been a welshed chit.

Sheriff Keirsey offered perhaps the soundest rebuttal to that idea. "If you seem to be welshing on a gambling debt," Keirsey told Trillin, "the first thing they want to do is put some hurt on you—break your legs, smash up your face, do some odds and ends. If they do have to kill you, they'd make it obvious, to leave a message."

Jenkins' fate could not be read in the physical evidence at the boat ramp. His gold Mercedes coupe was parked at the river. Its left rear tire was flat and the passenger-side door was open. Jenkins' wallet lay nearby, empty save for the victim's social security card. His Rolex watch was gone, as were his credit cards and an estimated $500 in cash he was thought to be carrying in his wallet that day. Many of those who think he was murdered believe the motive was money and that the killer, in all probability, was a stranger.

Their reasoning seemed sound, except to Sheriff Keirsey. Yet no theory of Johnny Jenkins' violent death can be considered without reference to certain other curious and poorly understood features of his business life. These include multiple fires and forgeries. Jenkins-owned establishments were hit by conflagrations three times—in 1969, 1985, and in 1987. He collected a $3.5 million insurance settlement after the 1985 blaze. The 1987 fire was ruled an arson, although no suspect was ever named. The forgeries were a more complicated matter.

According to investigations undertaken in the main by Texas printer and bookseller, Tom Taylor, beginning probably in the late 1970s some one or more people produced and sold a variety of forged documents, most of them "Texana," having to so with the state's history, government and culture. The bogus documents included at least 20 copies of the 1836 Texas Declaration of Independence. Some sold for $40,000 and more. One of the fake Declarations found its way into the Dallas Public Library's collection.

Former Texas governor Bill Clements bought another. Yale University acquired at least two of the forged documents.

Book man Tom Taylor's detective work brought him in time to the state of Mississippi and Pass Christian, a tiny hamlet where he found C. Dorman David, a onetime Houston rare-document dealer, former heroin addict and ex-con who quickly owned up to his role in the fakery. David, who also once had been Johnny Jenkins' partner in an Austin western-art gallery, admitted forging several historical documents, including the Texas Declaration of Independence.

But he also claimed that he had no intention of every selling the fakes. Instead, insisted David, he meant to sell the documents, marked as reproductions, to institutions that could not afford the real thing. This would be part of an effort to also establish himself as an expert on forgeries.

The fact that the forgeries were later discovered, he told reporter Lisa Belkin of The New York Times, demonstrated the truth of his claim.

"I'm an artist," David told Belkin. "I believe in my heart that if I wanted to I could make something no one could detect."

There were those who doubted C. Dorman David. And it was not at all clear if there were other sources of the bogus papers. What is known is that several people bought and sold them, and benefited from the trade.

Tom Taylor succeeded in establishing the provenance of 36 forgeries.

Five had been sold by David. Nine others were traced to a Houston dealer, William Simpson, who had no knowledge that they were fakes. The remainder, 22 forgeries in all, were sold by Johnny Jenkins.

No criminal charges ever have been filed in connection with any of the forgeries, and apparently no prosecutions are anticipated. Conspiracy theorists might argue this is because the one person who probably knew most about the case is now dead. On the other hand, no one publicly connected with the forgeries—either as a winner or a loser—appears to have been a viable suspect in Jenkins's death.

According to Sheriff Keirsey's analysis, the fires and forgeries played a subtle, indirect role in Johnny Jenkins' demise. By early 1989, there was plenty of speculation about his practices circulating within the small, clubby world of rare-book dealers, many of whom disliked Jenkins purely on account of his style.

The world at large wasn't acting any friendlier, either. In the spring of 1989, the Federal Deposit Insurance Corporation sued Jenkins for $1.3 million in connection with a loan he secured using his oil-rig operation as collateral. An Austin bank had foreclosed on his combination warehouse and bookstore, and he could look forward to the humiliation of having his property sold at public auction.

Hence the Keirsey theory. "His esteem and his prestige and his status had diminished in the last year," said the sheriff, "and he couldn't live with the stigma of defeat. His family says he was always able to pull out, but pretty soon you use your coupons up."

There'd be less dispute over Con Keirsey's conclusions had there been traces of gunpowder detected on Johnny Jenkins' hand. There weren't. And although that doesn't disprove the sheriff's argument, it is consistent with another troublesome detail; the death weapon has not been recovered. How can a person shoot himself in the back of the head, and then hide the weapon? One possibility, a bit of a far fetch, is that Jenkins had tied the weapon to a large perforated plastic bottle. After firing the fatal bullet, he dropped the gun, which was carried downstream by the bottle until it filled and sank taking the gun to the bottom with it.

It is also distinctly possible that Jenkins did nothing of the kind, that he simply shot himself and dropped the gun in the water where, despite searchers' best efforts, it remains.

Stranger things have happened.

One thing that almost everyone agrees upon about Johnny Jenkins' death is that he would have been tickled giddy to attract so much attention. The deed, whoever did it, also helped rescue Jenkins' businesses, since his lenders all had insurance policies on his life. The warehouse/bookstore that was about to be auctioned instead became the property of the Jenkins Company, without attachments. From this perspective, Johnny Jenkins' death may have been the best deal he ever did.

There is vigorous dissent. "People say, 'Oh, it's Johnny's last scam,'" said Michael Parrish, an employee and admirer. Parrish, who believed his boss was murdered, said he resented the suggested that Jenkins engineered the whole episode. "They say, 'He pulled the wool over everyone's eyes. He's up there laughing.' But it's hard to laugh when you're dead."

Reprinted from *Murders Among Us*

The Revolutionary

Back in the late 1960s and early 1970s, the Black Liberation Army was a fierce and tight-knit underground organization of self-styled urban guerrillas who cast themselves as radical warriors in the fight against white exploitation and oppression in the United States.

Law enforcement agencies demurred. Noting that the group's principal activities included bank robberies and armored-car heists, the cops regarded the Black Liberation Army as a fancy term for a bunch of violence-prone thugs.

The BLA's animating force—their "soul" as The New York Times put it—was Joanne Chesimard. A former Black Panther, her public life as a revolutionary blossomed in 1971 when Chesimard, then 34, was alleged to have taken part in an April 5 stickup at the Hilton Hotel in New York City. She later was implicated in BLA bank jobs in the Bronx and Queens, New York, as well.

Then the charges grew more serious. Early in 1973, Chesimard was accused in the attempted murder of a Queens policeman (this allegation later was dropped) and also of participating in the abduction and murder of a New York drug dealer. She was tried and acquitted of kidnap, and never brought to trial for the homicide.

That spring, Chesimard achieved enduring infamy (or fame, as some fellow radicals understand it) by taking part in the murder of a New Jersey state trooper.

After dark on May 2, she was driving south on the New Jersey turnpike in a white Pontiac with her lover, James Coston, also known as Zayd Shakur. Coston previously had acted as information minister for the Black Panthers.

Also in the Pontiac was Clark Squires, who answered to

Sundiata Acoli. New Jersey state trooper James M. Harper, twenty-nine, later testified that he pulled Chesimard over after noticing that her headlights weren't working properly. When he asked for her identification, said the trooper, Chesimard pulled a handgun. She has denied this.

Whoever's telling the truth, there is no doubt that a gun battle ensued. Harper was wounded while another trooper, thirty-four year old Werner Foerster, was killed. Coston-Shakur also died in the shoot-out.

Chesimard, whom police records indicate was armed that evening with a Browning nine-millimeter automatic, a .38-caliber Llama and a .38-caliber Browning automatic, sustained gunshot wounds in her chest, collarbone and arm.

Two months later, while awaiting trial, she smuggled a tape recording, entitled "To My People," from her cell. In it, Chesimard apologized for the incident as an example of her poor revolutionary discipline.

"I should have known better," she said on the tape, which was aired on radio stations and played at militants' gatherings. "The turnpike is a checkpoint where black people are stopped, searched, harassed and assaulted. Revolutionaries must never be in too much of a hurry or make careless decisions. He who runs when the sun is sleeping will stumble many times."

Chesimard reaffirmed her radicalism, proclaiming "war on the rich who prosper on our poverty, the politicians who lie to us with smiling faces and all the mindless, heartless robots who protect them and their property."

About six months later, in an anteroom of the Federal courthouse in Queens where she faced trial on one of her old bank robbery charges, Joanne Chesimard and a mystery companion conceived a child. The little girl, named Kakuya, weighed six pounds at birth on September 11, 1974, in the prison ward of the Elmhurst Hospital Center in Queens. Three years later, her mother was convicted of trooper Foerster's murder in a New Brunswick, New Jersey, court and was sentenced to a life term plus sixty-five years.

As is usual for long-term inmates, Chesimard routinely was moved from prison to prison over the coming years. In April of 1979, she was transferred from a Federal facility in West Virginia to the Clinton Correctional Institution for Women, a medium-security prison in the hills of western New Jersey, about fifteen miles east of the Pennsylvania border.

At Clinton, she was housed with six other women in a maximum-security structure known as South Hall, a one-story, yellow-brick building enclosed by a chain-link fence topped with two feet of barbed wire.

On Friday, November 2 of that year, a male visitor arrived at Clinton and checked into the registration building. He was not searched, but was escorted by prison van to South Hall and admitted within, where he met with Ms. Chesimard in a glass-enclosed booth.

Then two more male visitors arrived. They were not searched, either.

Instead, the same guard who escorted the first visitor to South Hall drove the new callers to the cellblock's front door. There, one of the two produced a gun and took the guard as his prisoner.

Inside, the man visiting Chesimard drew two handguns and directed the female guard standing outside the booth to open the door. All six people—Chesimard, her three visitors and the two guards—took the prison van across a wide field to the neighboring Hunterdon State School for the Mentally Handicapped.

In the parking lot were two women waiting with two vehicles; a Ford Maverick and a blue sedan. The guards were freed unharmed. Chesimard and her liberators fled in the getaway cars to Interstate 78, about 200 yards from the prison gates, and headed west into Pennsylvania.

As she later explained in her 1987 book, "Assata," Chesimard then secretly worked her way south along the

Atlantic coast with the aid of the Black Panther underground. Her first destination was Florida, then Central America and, finally, Fidel Castro's workers' paradise, Cuba in 1984, where she was accorded political asylum.

Now known as Assata Shakur, Chesimard has been reunited with her daughter in Cuba. Three years ago, she was the subject of a documentary film, "The Eyes of the Rainbow." She also has granted periodic interviews.

"Exile means separation from people I love," she told Christian Parenti, a sociology teacher at the New College of California in San Francisco. "I didn't and don't miss the U.S. per se. But black culture, black life in the U.S., that African-American flavor I definitely miss. The language, the movement, the style. I get nostalgic about that."

The interview did not touch on Shakur's reason for being in Cuba in the first place, that murder conviction back in New Jersey, where she is the state's most wanted fugitive. In 1998, after she granted an interview to New York City's WNBC-TV, an incensed New Jersey governor Christine Todd Whitman demanded that Castro send the fugitive back. Whitman also has posted a $25,000 reward for Shakur's return.

As long as Castro survives in Cuba, Shakur apparently is secure, no matter what demands U.S. politicians might make. But Fidel is in his 70s, and anything might occur with his death.

The Joanne Chesimard story is not yet over.

Reprinted from *Wanted for Murder*

Hollow Men

It's boom time for aberrant crime.

From the killer kids in Colorado to a homicidal janitor at Yosemite, around America with serial "Railway Killer" Angel Maturino Resendez, and down to Mark Barton's day-trader hell in Atlanta, 1999 so far has been a banner year for murderous moral imbeciles. Even a deranged bigot named Buford O. Furrow, Jr., made the TV news recently for hunting Jews, and killing an Hispanic letter carrier.

It's tempting to view these bloody outbreaks as inter-changeable pieces of the same disturbing puzzle; a country inexplicably under siege not by armies, or even gangs, but by mostly middle class white guys of varying ages who are skidding wildly out of control, targeting multiple defenseless victims, usually strangers, for murder.

In fact, though the net effect may be the same, there is a world of deviant difference between deeply troubled shooters such as Eric Harris and Dylan Klebold at Columbine High, and sexually-motivated ritual predators like Resendez, who has been charged in four states with nine serial murders and one rape (and is rumored to have had post-mortem sex with at least one of his other female victims), or Cary Stayner, who is accused of brutally dispatching four females at Yosemite, two by strangulation, and two by slitting their throats, decapitating one, and nearly decapitating the other.

San Diego forensic psychiatrist Dr. Park Elliott Dietz has shown that most mass murders (defined by the FBI as "a homicide involving four or more victims in one location and within one event") are committed by the depressed and the paranoid, who see themselves as agents, even heroes, of retribution, angrily lashing out at a world they fear and hate. If they survive going postal (and few of them do) Dr. Dietz reports mass killers are uniformly disappointed to discover the experience doesn't solve, but actually intensifies, their psychic pain. Moreover, for all the bloody drama, mass murder is a copycat crime. These killers take their inspiration from each other, all variations on an original theme by Charles Joseph Whitman, the University of Texas tower shooter who invented modern mass murder 33 years ago.

Not so the self-realizing ritualistic killer, who selects for cunning, psychopathology and hyper narcissism. Above all, this killer savors his work, obsesses on it, keeps souvenirs, and sometimes detailed records. He is not in pain; he causes it. His need exceeds sex and violence. It is a pathological desire for complete mastery; he wants to engulf and to annihilate a victim. As the serial killer Ted Bundy told us nearly 20 years ago on Death Row in Florida, the thrill in sexual homicide comes with "possessing" victims "physically as one would possess a potted plant, a painting or a Porsche. Owning, as it were, this individual."

This little-appreciated particularity in the ritualistic killer's psyche is central to his crimes, and distinguishes him from every other criminal, deviant or otherwise. Roy Hazelwood, a former FBI profiler and specialist in sexual criminals now retired from the Bureau's Behavioral Science Unit, says it was Harvey Glatman, L.A.'s so-called Lonely Hearts Killer of the 1950s, who first illustrated this truth to him.

Studying Glatman (who was executed in 1959), Hazelwood puzzled over his habit of first incapacitating his victims in their apartments, then binding them and transporting them out into the desert, where Glatman finally killed them. "He could have raped and killed these women in their apartments," says Hazelwood. "But Glatman kept them alive at increased risk to himself. I realized that the enjoyment he took made the risk worth it to him. I later understood that enjoyment, that sense of possession, is power to the ritualistic offender, and total possession is absolute power."

All sexual crime is driven by fantasy—Cary Stayner told a reporter he'd been dreaming of killing women for 30 years, since he was seven—and because no two serial killers share exactly the same murder fantasy, possession means something different to each of them, too.

Bundy, for example, desired a lifeless female form—comatose or dead. Just before his 1989 execution, Ted admitted to police detectives that he kept some of his victims in such a state for hours and days before disposing of them. Various of his 30 or so victims were buried in shallow woodland graves, where he sometimes revisited them. One who was found frozen in the mountains of Utah appeared to have received a post-mortem shampoo.

Another was given a fresh application of make-up before Bundy discarded her body. "If you've got time, they can be anyone you want them to be," he later told FBI agent Bill Hagmaier, who came to know Ted intimately while interviewing him in the 1980s.

Ted explained to the agent that "murder isn't just a crime of lust or violence. It becomes possession. They are part of you.... You feel the last bit of breath leaving their bodies.... You're looking into their eyes.... A person in that situation is God!"

Bundy even photographed his victims, and kept a stash of their skulls in his Seattle apartment. "When you work hard to do something right," he said, "you don't want to forget it."

For Mike DeBardeleben, a sexual sadist who is spending the balance of his days in Federal prison for crimes various as counterfeiting and rape-abduction, possession meant a live victim, suffering under his control.

"There is no greater power over another person than that of inflicting pain on her," DeBardeleben wrote in his private journal. "To force her to undergo suffering without her being

able to defend herself. The pleasure in the constant domina-
tion over another person is the very essence of the sadistic
drive."

John Wayne Gacy asserted total command of his young
male victims by burying most of them directly under his
house. They literally were arrayed beneath his feet.

Jeffrey Dahmer went so far as to physically consume his
victims—complete possession, total annihilation—as did
California serial killer Edmund Kemper, who sliced a bit of
one girl's leg into a macaroni casserole.

Experts describe possession as something familiar to us
all—possessiveness—taken to it's pathological extreme.
"Along the continuum of sexual behavior from an innocent
kiss to rape-murder," says Robert E. Freeman-Longo, a
leading authority on sexual abuse and former director of the
Sex Offender Treatment at Oregon State Hospital, possessiveness is first noticeable among intimate, consenting
sexual partners, such as married couples. Possession at this
level is really jealousy.

"When the behavior is pathological, you don't see
possession associated with so-called nuisance crimes, such
as exposing yourself or voyeurism, where the only contact is
visual. Among rapists you may see a practical need for
momentary control, but it's the high-end guys, sadists and
rape-killers where insecurity turns to anger and this idea of
possession comes into play."

"They take the objectification of women to a
pathological extreme," agrees forensic psychologist J. Reid
Meloy, author of a standard text on deviant criminal
behavior, The psychopathic Mind. The key to understanding
possession, says Meloy, is narcissism.

"We know from the research that psychopaths have a
core, aggressive narcissism that is fundamental to their
personality. If you remove that narcissism, you don't have a
psychopath."

One hallmark of the narcissist is lack of empathy; they

are psychically insulated from those around them. Another is grandiosity. The charismatic and handsome Bundy, arguably the first celebrity serial killer, cemented his image in the public mind by playing to the press at every opportunity, and by acting as his own attorney. Both Angel Resendez and Cary Stayner commented on their cases to reporters, contrary to their attorneys' advice, soon after their arrests last summer.

Stayner told Ted Rowlands of KBWB-TV in San Francisco how he'd skillfully thrown the FBI off his trail after his first three homicides in February. "When you outwit the police, it reinforces your grandiose fantasies," says Meloy—even when you're a serial killer manqué.

Henry Lee Lucas, the snaggle-toothed drifter with an IQ in the 80s who may have killed three people, claimed at one time to have murdered more than 600, and easily conned the Texas Rangers into believing such an inadequate low-life was by far the most prolific serial killer of all time.

"That was a marvelous example of psychopathic manipulation," says Meloy. "Lucas was able to prove he was smarter and shrewder than this notable law enforcement agency."

Angel Resendez, who may not score much higher on a standard IQ test than Lucas, wrote the San Antonio Express-News a three-page letter. In it, he said he'd turned himself in out of love for his infant daughter, a patently absurd claim for a serial bludgeon killer. In a second, 11-page letter to KTRK-TV in Houston, the self-dramatizing Resendez wrote ominously of his "enemy," a scary "creature" inside of him. "I've been fighting this creature all of my life," Resendez reported, "and now I know it is me, so I fear, yes I fear and shake."

Along with obsessively seeking others' awed or admiring attention, the narcissist also believes himself omniscient and even omnipotent. "You can see how control of another person would stimulate those fantasies," observes Meloy.

The narcissist feels entitled, and when he is thwarted, he acts out, just as young children, who are supremely narcissistic, act out. "Think of a toddler raging against an object that won't do what he wants," says Meloy. "I have this image in my mind of a two-year-old squeezing a puppy's feet. He's attempting to control the animal's behavior, and probably deriving some pleasure from that.''

Among adult narcissistic destroyers, the principal animating influence is the green monster—envy. "The wish to destroy goodness is probably the simplest definition of envy," says Meloy. "These guys often have pretty barren lives in terms of what we call 'good objects,' and they want to damage or destroy the goodness they cannot have. They need to make the almost intolerable feeling of envy go away, so they take a woman and defile and devalue her, like Bundy plucking the young flowers of the upper middle class.

"If you can do that completely, she wasn't worth having in the first place, and you've removed the cause for envy."

Unlike mass killers, sexual killers find the act of murder itself—not just its objective—profoundly gratifying. Janet Warren, a frequent research collaborator with Roy Hazelwood and a faculty member at the University of Virginia's Department of Behavioral Medicine and Psychiatry, recalls one sexual sadist she studied in particular.

"His first killing turned out to be a male hitchhiker," says Warren, "with whom he was competing for rides on the freeway. He described raising a stone above his head and beginning to crash it down on the man's head. He had an incredible feeling of exhilaration.

"Then when he started killing women, he actually breathed life back into a couple of them, because they lost consciousness too quickly. He said, 'I wasn't going to let myself be robbed of the experience. I wanted to see in her eyes that she knew she was going to die, and that I was going to take her life. It is only in having that reflected back at me—and I need a conscious person to do that—that I can experience the power and control of being God-like."

Central to possession is the necessity to utterly dehumanize the victim, typified by a comment from Robert Leroy Anderson, a sexual killer now on Death Row in South Dakota. According to an acquaintance, Anderson once complained that his first murder victim, a female fellow employee at a meat-packing plant in Sioux Falls, proved less than ideal for his purposes because he knew her too well and could not completely objectify her. It was therefore impossible to fully incorporate her into his fantasy.

"The perpetrator cannot see the victim as a separate, whole, real, meaningful person, with her own thoughts and feelings and perceptions," says Meloy. "She must be reduced to an object with no meaning except to gratify his desires."

Janet Warren says the thrill lies in consuming and sexually eradicating the victim-as-possession.

"It is interesting that Dahmer ate people, but that was part of the same thing. For instance, decapitating a woman. Taking off a person's head is so destructive. He is saying, 'You will be nothing. You will have no individuality.'"

Such behavior, of course, is primitive, particularly necrophagia; Hannibal Lecter isn't as sophisticated as he seems. For all his slyness, creativity and rich fantasy life—all often taken as tokens of intelligence—the sexual killer may be more complex than a two year old squeezing the puppy's feet, but he is no more highly evolved.

And because he is incomplete, this killer isn't just taking what he envies, he's trying to steal what he lacks—a core. Figuratively, literally or symbolically, he keeps trying, in vain, to fill himself up.

"These men," says Warren, "have to take women as slaves, or as dinner or as a destroyed object. They can have no ambiguity, ambivalence, confusion, vulnerability, intense anger, fear or love in their lives. All that is fundamental to human intimacy is destroyed by what they do. But I think they have to do it that way, because they can't handle any of those experiences.

They have to do it that way because they are empty.

"That, by the way, is how they often describe themselves. Empty."

Reprinted from Salon.com

Other True Crime Titles
from Authorlink Press

<u>Investigation/Research</u>

Serial Murder
Future Implications for Police Investigations
Robert D. Keppel, Ph.D.

In this essential guide for criminal justice professionals, an expert homicide investigator and researcher explores the daunting task of investigating serial murders. Robert D. Keppel presents five detailed profiles of savage killers, to demonstrate how the smallest procedural detail can assure or wreck successful prosecution, and suggests how investigators can plug the loopholes. Dr. Keppel is president of the Institute for Forensics in Seattle, and former longtime chief criminal investigator.

> *"…an excellent analysis of police operations and the legal dilemmas and consequences that occurred in a series of high profile prosecutions."*

> Vernon J. Geberth, Author of
> *Practical Homicide Investigation:*
> *Tactics, Procedures, and Forensic Techniques*

<u>Investigation/Research</u>

Criminal Shadows
Innre Narratives of Evil
David Canter, Ph.D.

Britain's leading pioneer in the psychological science of criminal profiling reveals how vicious serial killers and rapists unconsciously cast shadows of their identity at the crime scene. The telltale patterns, when scientifically understood, can help police capture these brutal offenders.

Criminal Shadows leads the reader through Dr. Canter's breakthrough profiling techniques, now adopted by a growing number of police forces throughout the world. A must read for anyone in the field of criminal justice. The updated paperback edition is now available for the first time in the USA by Authorlink Press, after a successful run by HarperCollins in the UK.

True Crime

Ted Bundy:
Conversations With A Killer
The Death Row Interviews
Stephen G. Michaud
and Hugh Aynesworth

The interviews that chilled the nation in the 1980s, are again available in this updated edition. Drawn from more than 150 hours of taped interviews by authors Stephen G. Michaud and Hugh Aynesworth, *Conversations With A Killer* takes readers inside the mind of one of the best-known serial killers of the past 100 years.

The Only Living Witness
The True Story of Serial
Sex Killer Ted Bundy
Stephen G. Michaud
and Hugh Aynesworth

The Only Living Witness, best selling story of serial sex killer Ted Bundy again is available through major bookstores and online booksellers. The updated True Crime Classic features a new foreword by FBI profiler Roy Hazelwood. Selected by *The New York Daily News* as one of the ten best true crime books ever written.

9 781928 704225

90000